Review, Practice, & Mastery of

COMMON CORE

ENGLISH LANGUAGE ARTS

STATE STANDARDS

Reviewers

Amy Barr • Park Hill School District • Park Hill, MO

Tracie Baumgartner • Valley View School District • Bolingbrook, IL

Barbara Burns • Lammersville Unified School District • Mountain House, CA

Karen Cooke • Cobb County School District • Marietta, GA

Amy Corr • Douglas County School District • Highlands Ranch, CO

Rachel Nichols • Lower Merion School District • Ardmore, PA

Arlene Peters • Orange County Public Schools • Orlando, FL

Brian Selling • Community Day Charter School • Lawrence, MA

Kim Sheehy • Sauquoit Valley Central Schools • Sauquoit, NY

Beverly Smith • Corona-Norco Unified School District • Ontario, CA

Colleen Thomas • Sandwich Public Schools • Sandwich, MA

Holly Walker • Whitman-Hanson Regional School District • Hanson, MA

© 2013 **Perfection Learning®**
www.perfectionlearning.com

5 6 EB 16 15 14 13

EB/Ann Arbor, MI, USA
06/13

94637
ISBN-10: 0-7891-8314-5
ISBN-13: 978-0-7891-8314-9

Printed in the United States of America

To the Student

This book will help you review, practice, and master the English Language Arts Common Core State Standards. Here are the steps to follow to use this book.

1. Take the Tryout Test over Reading Literature, Reading Informational Text, and Language and check your answers. Use the chart below to find out your strengths and weaknesses in the areas covered. Remember the questions that are hard for you to answer. These will be the types of questions you need to work on the most.

2. Work through the units that follow the Tryout Test. The lessons in each unit review example items and provide a practice test based on the standards. Fill in the Keeping Score chart on page 143 as you complete each practice test.

3. After completing all the lessons, take the Mastery Test. Your score on this test will show your understanding of the Common Core Standards.

4. Work through the Writing Test Workshop section of the book. These lessons will help you learn how to read a writing prompt and how to get your ideas down on paper in a clear and organized manner.

Reading Literature	Tryout Test Items	Mastery Test Items
Unit One—Key Ideas and Details		
Lesson 1 Cite, Infer, and Summarize	3, 7, 15, 19	7, 8, 10
Lesson 2 Character and Theme	1, 2, 5, 17	1, 2, 3, 4, 16
Unit Two—Craft and Structure		
Lesson 3 Word Choice	4, 8, 11, 16	6, 9, 13
Lesson 4 Structure	12, 13	14, 17
Lesson 5 Point of View	14	5, 12
Reading Informational Text	**Tryout Test Items**	**Mastery Test Items**
Unit Three—Key Ideas and Details		
Lesson 6 Cite, Infer, and Summarize	20, 21, 24	21, 23, 36, 37
Lesson 7 Supporting Details	23, 28, 29	22, 24
Unit Four—Craft and Structure		
Lesson 8 Structure and Point of View	27, 30	18, 29, 35
Lesson 9 Visual Formats	22, 25	19, 20
Unit Five—Integration of Knowledge and Ideas		
Lesson 10 Reasons and Evidence	26, 33, 34, 35, 36	28, 30, 31, 32
Lesson 11 Conflicting Texts	31, 32	33, 34
Language	**Tryout Test Items**	**Mastery Test Items**
Unit Six—Conventions of Standard English		
Lesson 12 Grammar and Usage	37, 38, 39, 40, 41, 42, 50	38, 39, 40, 41, 42, 43, 44, 45
Lesson 13 Capitalization, Punctuation, and Spelling	43, 44, 45, 46, 47, 48, 49	46, 47, 48, 49, 50
Unit Seven—Vocabulary		
Lesson 14 Context Clues and Reference Materials	9, 18	11, 26, 27
Lesson 15 Word Parts and Relationships	6, 10	15, 25

Table of Contents

continued

Unit Four—Craft and Structure

Unit Five—Integration of Knowledge and Ideas

Language

Unit Six—Conventions of Standard English

Unit Seven—Vocabulary

Writing

Standards Key: RL = Reading Literature, RI = Reading Informational Text,
L = Language, W = Writing, RH = Reading Standards for Literacy in History/Social Studies,
RST = Reading Standards for Literacy in Science/Technical Studies, WHST = Writing Standards
for Literacy in History/Social Studies, Science, and Technical Subjects

Note: A complete correlation of the Grade 8 Common Core State Standards for English Langauge
Arts can be found in the Grade 8 Teacher Guide.

Tryout Test: Part 1   Estimated time: 50 minutes

Directions: Read the passage. Then answer the questions that follow.

Blockhead and the Queen Bee

Once upon a time, there were three brothers. The youngest was called Blockhead because his brothers considered him stupid. One day, the three set off in search of adventure.

Along the way, the brothers came upon a huge anthill. "Let's stir this up and see what happens," said the eldest brother.

Blockhead frowned and said, "Oh, leave the poor creatures alone. They've done you no harm."

His two brothers laughed, but went on their way without bothering the ants. A bit farther down the road, they chanced upon a lake in which many ducks were diving and swimming. The middle brother said, "Let's snare a few ducks and roast them for dinner."

Again Blockhead protested. "Leave the poor creatures alone. I'll not let you harm them."

His brothers shook their heads and made fun of their stupid brother, but they went on their way without bothering the ducks. However, before long, they reached a tree with honey dripping from a huge hive. The eldest brother looked thoughtfully at the tree. "Let's set fire to this hive to suffocate the bees and steal their honey," he suggested.

Blockhead was outraged. "Leave the poor creatures alone," he said. "I will not let them come to harm."

Once again, Blockhead's brothers laughed at his soft heart, saying that it reflected his soft head. But they headed off without carrying out their threat. Soon afterward, the three brothers came upon a huge, deserted castle. They walked through the unguarded gate, crossed the empty courtyard, and then roamed from room to room until they reached a door with an iron grate.

"Look!" cried the eldest brother, "I can see a little man in there." He banged on the door and shouted, "Let us in, old fellow!"

The old man approached slowly. Silently, he unlocked the door and led the three brothers to a table heaped with food. They ate and ate. Then they fell asleep on the chamber floor.

The next morning, the brothers woke to find the old man—still silent—standing and staring at them.

The eldest brother stretched, yawned, and said, "Oh, it is you, old man. What do you want?"

The old man didn't say a word. He just handed the eldest brother a stone tablet.

"Let's see," said the eldest brother. "It says that I must complete three tasks in order to free this castle from an evil enchantment. Well, that sounds interesting enough."

"What are the tasks?" asked the second brother.

"This only lists the first," his brother replied. "I am to find the Princess's pearls in the woods. That seems simple enough. I will be off now and back in time for dinner."

As instructed, the eldest brother searched the woods around the castle. However, by dusk, he had found only a few pearls. He returned and handed them to the old man, saying, "This task was impossible. So tell me what the second task is and perhaps I will do that tomorrow."

The old man just shook his head. At once, the eldest brother turned to stone.

The next day, the old man appeared again at the chamber door. He handed the middle brother the stone tablet.

"Well," said the middle brother to Blockhead, "I am to do the same task. I am sure I can succeed where our brother failed. After all, I am the cleverest of the three of us."

So the middle brother headed into the forest, whistling merrily. He did not return until after the sun had set. In his hand he held only a few pearls.

"No one can complete this foolish task," he complained. "Why I—"

With a shake of his head, the old man interrupted. And at once the middle brother was turned to stone.

Now, Blockhead knew that his turn was next. He would have to find the pearls or be turned to stone. "What will I do?" he moaned. "I am only a soft-hearted blockhead. If my clever brothers could not complete this task, how can I succeed?"

That night Blockhead hardly closed his eyes, so worried was he about being turned to stone. So he was awake when the old man appeared at the chamber door with the stone tablet. Sighing, Blockhead trudged into the forest to find the pearls.

For several hours, he turned over logs and rocks, hoping to find a few pearls. However, he had little luck. "I have searched and searched," he said, "but these pearls are hard to find. I will be turned to stone like my brothers. Oh, woe is me!"

In despair, Blockhead sat on a rock and started to weep. Then, through his sobs, he heard a tiny voice. "Stop your weeping. You saved my kingdom, so now we shall help you."

To Blockhead's amazement, thousands of ants started to scurry toward him along the mossy forest floor. In minutes, a huge heap of pearls lay at Blockhead's feet, shining like stars in a mossy sky. Smiling, Blockhead headed back to the castle.

When he arrived, Blockhead marched right up to the silent old man. "Here are the pearls," he said. "Now, tell me, what is my next task?"

The old man handed him a second stone tablet. Slowly, Blockhead made out the words.

"Hmmm . . . I must search the lake for the key to the Princess's room. Very well. I can do that."

At once, Blockhead left the castle and headed for the lake. When he reached the shore, the ducks he had saved earlier dived to the bottom of the lake and retrieved the key.

Blockhead took the key back and presented it to the little man, who used it to unlock a heavy door. Behind the door, three lovely princesses lay in a deep sleep.

Without a word, the old man handed Blockhead another stone tablet. Blockhead studied it, curious about his third and last task.

"I see," he said. "I must identify which of the princesses is the youngest. But they look exactly alike!"

Then Blockhead read on. "Ah, here is a clue. It tells me what each maiden ate before being enchanted. The oldest had sugar, the second had syrup, and the youngest had honey."

Blockhead stared and stared at the lovely <u>trio</u>, thinking about the clue. Then he had an idea. "I shall call the queen of the bees, whose lives I saved. *She* will be able to tell which princess ate honey!"

And that is what happened. The queen bee flew straight to the lips of the youngest princess—the one with invisible traces of honey on her lips.

At once, the enchantment was broken and the castle and everyone in it came to life— even Blockhead's two brothers. Blockhead married the youngest princess and his brothers married her sisters. And they all lived happily together.

GO ON

1   What is the theme of this passage?

   A Complete tasks on time or you will be punished.

   B The older you are, the wiser you are likely to be.

   C Kindness is often returned.

   D Family members must stick together.

2   The element of enchantment in this story is a clue that the passage is an example of what type of literature?

   A myth

   B folktale

   C trickster tale

   D tall tale

3   Based on his actions, we can infer that Blockhead is what kind of person?

   A kind and good

   B foolish and simple

   C wise and ambitious

   D lazy and cruel

4   Read this excerpt from the passage.

> . . . a huge heap of pearls lay at Blockhead's feet, shining like stars in a mossy sky . . .

The author compares the pearls to stars in order to—

   A suggest that each pearl is enormous.

   B show that the moss on the ground looks like the sky.

   C draw attention to how the pearls gleam with light.

   D create the idea that Blockhead's feet are in the sky.

5   The two oldest brothers are turned into stone because—

   A the old man likes the youngest brother best.

   B they eat all of the enchanted food.

   C they are thoughtless and cruel.

   D they cannot find all the princess's pearls.

6   The prefix *tri-* as used in the word <u>trio</u> means—

   A three

   B before

   C over

   D not

7 Write a summary of the story. Include only the main events. (3 points)

_____

_____

_____

_____

_____

_____

_____

Directions: Read the poem and answer the questions that follow.

from The Village Blacksmith
by Henry Wadsworth Longfellow

Under a spreading chestnut-tree
   The village smithy stands;
The smith, a mighty man is he,
   With large and sinewy hands.
And the muscles of his brawny arms
   Are strong as iron bands.

His hair is crisp, and black, and long,
   His face is like the tan;
His brow is wet with honest sweat,
   He earns whate'er he can,
And looks the world in the face,
   For he owes not any man.

Week in, week out, from morn till night,
   You hear his bellows blow;
You can hear him swing his heavy sledge,
   With measured beat and slow,

Like a sexton ringing the village bell,
   When the evening sun is low.

* * *

Toiling—rejoicing—sorrowing;
   Onward through life he goes;
Each morning sees some task begin,
   Each evening sees it close;
Something attempted, something done,
   Has earned a night's <u>repose</u>.

Thanks, thanks, to thee, my worthy friend,
   For the lesson thou has taught!
Thus at the flaming forge of life
   Our fortunes must be wrought;
Thus on the sounding anvil shaped
   Each burning deed and thought.

GO ON

8 The poet makes an analogy between the blacksmith's hard work and—

   A honest sweat.

   B an individual's deeds and thoughts.

   C the spreading chestnut tree.

   D ringing a bell.

9 As used in the poem, what does the word <u>repose</u> mean?

   A work   **C** rest

   B do over   **D** reward

10 Finish the following word analogy.

   CARPENTER : HAMMER :: Blacksmith :

   A sledge   **C** horse

   B forge   **D** hands

11 The poet uses words such as *mighty, honest,* and *worthy* to create a tone of—

   A surprise.

   B suspicion.

   C jealousy.

   D approval.

12 What impact does using poetry to describe the blacksmith have on readers?

   A The words and images of the poem appeal to readers' emotions.

   B The words present a true account of a blacksmith whom the poet knew.

   C The language will help explain what is involved in a blacksmith's job.

   D Poetry appeals to readers because it is short and easy to read.

Directions: Use both "Blockhead and the Queen Bee" and "The Village Blacksmith" to answer question 13.

13 How are the structures of "Blockhead and the Queen Bee" and "The Village Blacksmith" different? How do their different structures communicate the meaning of each work? Use examples from BOTH passages to support your answer. (3 points)

_____

_____

_____

_____

_____

_____

Directions: Read the passage and answer the questions that follow.

The Blue Sneakers

1   When Molly showed up for her first babysitting job with the Jacksons, she was imagining the light blue sneakers she would buy with the money she earned. The Jacksons had 7-year-old twin boys and a 14-month-old girl. Molly was a seasoned babysitter who had once watched five kids for a whole week. This job would be a piece of cake.

2   The kids were at the dining room table when Molly arrived. The twins, Sam and Paul, were dressed alike. "Sam can't eat a lot of sugar," Mrs. Jackson said, "so he has peaches for dessert. You and Paul can have the ice cream in the freezer." The dining room table was covered with crumpled napkins, broken crayons, and race cars, many of which seemed to be missing their wheels. Sam and Paul winked at each other as Mr. and Mrs. Jackson hurried out the door.

3   "Well," Molly said brightly, "let's eat!" The twins slurped their spaghetti while the baby, Susie, took a handful of cereal and launched it across the table. The twins cackled, and then Susie laughed and grabbed another handful of cereal. "If you stop laughing," Molly said, "she might stop throwing food." The twins briefly became serious, but when Susie heaved a glob of strained vegetables at them, they couldn't help laughing again. Milk spattered out of Paul's nose, and all three kids doubled over with choking laughter.

4   Molly wiped up as much of the mess as she could, and then served some ice cream and a bowl of peaches. She placed the peaches in front of Sam. "I'm not Sam!" he announced. "I'm Paul."

5   "Oh, sorry," Molly said, and gave the other twin the peaches. He told her in an even louder voice that he was Paul.

6   "Look," Molly said. "I can't tell you apart. Sam is not supposed to eat sugar. I trust Sam not to do anything that he's not supposed to do. Now, which one is Sam?"

7   "I am," the two boys said at the same time.

8   "Okay, forget it," Molly said. "No one will have any dessert."

9   The boys protested and then Susie started to cry. As her wails increased in volume, the boys grew louder as well. Molly sent the two of them to the living room to play while she took Susie to her room for a diaper change. As she was buttoning Susie's outfit, Molly heard the blender begin to whir and then an "oops" from the kitchen. The twins had started making their own dessert but had forgotten to put the top on the blender. It looked like a can of paint had exploded in the kitchen. The walls and the counters were covered with splattered milkshake.

10   Molly knew it was time to be tough. Frustrated, she took three deep breaths to calm herself and told the boys that if they watched a movie and went straight to bed, she wouldn't tell their parents about their insubordination. The boys grudgingly agreed and trotted off toward the family room. While they were occupied, Molly rocked Susie, singing her some lullabies. Soon, the baby was asleep in her arms.

11   "Let's go, Paul and Sam," she said, standing in the doorway of the family room with her hands on her hips. "It's time for bed."

12   "I'm not Paul," said one of the boys.

13   "And I'm not Sam," said the other.

14   "No more funny business," Molly cried.

15   "But I'm not Paul," one of the boys protested. "How can I go to bed if you don't tell me to go to bed?"

16   "I'm telling you both to go to bed," Molly insisted. "No more questions."

17   They giggled and trotted off toward their bedroom. Molly collapsed on the couch and closed her eyes.

18   When Molly cracked open her eyes, it was 10:50 p.m. The Jackson had said they would be home at 11 p.m. "The kitchen!" she thought. She feverishly wiped the sticky milkshake residue off the walls and cabinets. She had just put the sponge away when she heard the front door open.

19   "I hope the kids weren't any trouble," Mrs. Jackson said.

20   "Oh, they were no trouble at all!" said Molly, crossing her fingers behind her back. On the way home, she imagined how satisfying it would feel when she finally bought those light blue sneakers.

---

14 Why might Molly's experience seem humorous from the reader's point of view but frustrating from Molly's point of view? Use details from the story to support your answer. (3 points)

_____

_____

_____

_____

_____

15 What detail from the story helps you infer that Molly will be asked to babysit for the Jacksons again?

　　A Molly tells Mrs. Jackson that the boys were insubordinate.

　　B Molly crosses her fingers behind her back.

　　C Molly tells Mrs. Jackson that the kids were no trouble.

　　D Mrs. Jackson discovers the mess in the kitchen.

---

16 The phrase "This job would be a piece of cake" means—

   A the kids will be as sweet as cake.

   B the job will be easy.

   C Molly will give the kids cake for dessert.

   D the job will be messy.

17 Why does Molly decide not to give the twins dessert?

   A Sam is not supposed to eat a lot of sugar.

   B Susie starts to cry.

   C She wants to punish the twins for their bad behavior.

   D She cannot figure out which twin is Sam.

18 Use this sample dictionary entry for the word <u>season</u> to answer the question.

> **season** *v.* **1.** to add zest or interest to **2.** to make more suitable for use by aging or drying *adj.* **3.** flavored with spices **4.** experienced and skilled

Which definition best fits <u>seasoned</u> as it is used in paragraph 1?

   A definition 1

   B definition 2

   C definition 3

   D definition 4

19 How do Molly's actions during the babysitting job show what Molly is like? Use evidence from the story to explain Molly's character. (5 points)

_____

_____

_____

_____

_____

_____

Take a break. Then go on to Part 2.

Directions: Read the passage and answer the questions that follow.

A Hurricane's Destruction

1 In the last days of October 1998, Hurricane Mitch raged through Central America. The category five hurricane generated winds of 180 miles per hour and dumped several feet of rain. Newspapers worldwide presented facts and statistics about Mitch's destruction: More than 5,000 Hondurans drowned or died in landslides. A thousand miles of roads and at least 100 bridges were made unusable. The estimate of total damage was 5 billion dollars.

2 Facts and statistics such as these are certainly impressive. However, they reveal to us very little about how people are directly affected by natural disasters like hurricanes. Consider the following examples related to Hurricane Mitch.

3 In northern Honduras, people in one village on the Chamelecón River were accustomed to their houses being flooded during hurricane season. At such times, they would stay in temporary shelters they constructed on higher ground. Then, when the water level lowered, they would return home. But Mitch brought the villagers more than water. The extraordinary amount of rainfall caused landslides everywhere—perhaps as many as a million, according to one estimate. Long after Mitch had died out, several feet of mud from landslides remained in the homes of the villagers. Accustomed to being on their own, they immediately began digging and sweeping. Many weeks later, bulldozers finally arrived to speed up the work.

4 Tegucigalpa, the capital of Honduras, lies far inland. Tall mountains surround it. Despite its geographical position, the city did not escape Mitch's wrath. Entire neighborhoods slid down hills into the Choluteca River. The swollen river demolished other neighborhoods on its banks as well. In one working-class neighborhood, only a few of the more than 200 houses remained. Everyone in this neighborhood managed to escape to higher ground. But that was only the beginning of their problems. Wanting to relocate together, the families asked the city government to assist them. But help was slow in coming, and they began to lose hope. Finally, community leaders decided to act on their own to find a place to relocate. With the help of Michael Miller, a schoolteacher from the United States, they created a Web site and asked for donations. With the money received, the families were able to buy land outside the capital for new homes.

www.photos.com

5 The next time you read about a natural disaster, go beyond the facts and statistics. Many of the writers and journalists on the scene of the disaster describe the human drama, putting a face on the dollar figures so often used to describe the damage done.

Saffir-Simpson Scale[1]		
Category	**Wind Speed**	**Effects**
One	74–95 mph	little damage to buildings; trees and shrubs may be uprooted or damaged; some coastal flooding
Two	96–110 mph	damage to roofs and windows; serious damage to mobile homes, trees, and shrubs; flooding in coastal and low-lying areas
Three	111–130 mph	some structural damage to homes and buildings; destruction of mobile homes; flooding in low-lying areas may extend inland 8 miles or more
Four	131–155 mph	extensive damage to homes and buildings; major beach erosion; flooding of areas lower than 10 feet above sea level
Five	greater than 155 mph	complete destruction of many homes and buildings; flooding of areas less than 15 feet above sea level; buildings and trees may be blown great distances; massive evacuations may be required

[1] The scale was developed in 1969 by Herbert Saffir, an engineer, and Dr. Bob Simpson, director of the National Hurricane Center, to make the hazards of storms easier to communicate to emergency management teams.

20 Which sentence BEST summarizes the information in paragraph 1?

A In October 1998, Hurricane Mitch hit Central America and brought death and destruction to Honduras.

B In 1998, Hurricane Mitch, with winds of 180 miles per hour, dumped several feet of rain and caused landslides.

C Hurricane Mitch struck Central America in 1998 and did billions of dollars worth of damage.

D In late October 1998, newspapers printed stories about a huge hurricane that struck Central America.

21 What can you infer from reading this passage?

A Hurricanes rarely strike Honduras.

B Hurricanes are more common in Tegucigalpa than in other parts of Honduras.

C Hurricanes are not unusual in Honduras.

D Hurricane Mitch is the worst hurricane that has ever hit Honduras.

GO ON

22 What is the purpose of the chart that accompanies this passage?

   A It tells how forecasters predict hurricanes.
   B It compares hurricane wind speeds and potential damage.
   C It describes how hurricanes form.
   D It lists dangerous hurricanes of the last century.

23 What effect of Hurricane Mitch was most difficult for the people living in a village on the Chamelecón River?

   A the length of time they had to stay in temporary shelters
   B the strength of the wind
   C the mud left behind in their homes
   D the time it took the water level to lower

24 The author wrote this passage mainly to—

   A tell the human story behind the facts.
   B present facts and figures about the effects of Hurricane Mitch.
   C describe the cost of repairs needed because of Hurricane Mitch.
   D encourage the reader to pay less attention to facts and statistics.

25 The author describes Mitch as a "category five hurricane." According to information in the chart, a category five hurricane may cause—

   A little damage to buildings.
   B some coastal flooding.
   C damage to roofs and windows.
   D massive evacuations.

26 The author believes the people of Honduras are capable of helping themselves when natural disasters strike. Does the author provide sufficient evidence to support this viewpoint? Is the evidence relevant, or does he include unrelated details? Use details and examples from the passage to support your answer. (3 points)

_____

_____

_____

_____

_____

_____

_____

Directions: Read the passage and answer the questions that follow.

Pompeii and Vesuvius

www.photos.com

1   In 1748, near the city of Naples, a peasant was digging in a vineyard when he unearthed a section of buried wall. He had come upon a remnant of Pompeii, a city that had been buried under cinders, ashes, and stone for nearly 1,700 years.

2   Located on the southwest coast of what is now Italy, Pompeii was a bustling city with about 20,000 inhabitants, including wine and oil merchants, wealthy landowners, shopkeepers, artisans, and slaves. Then one day in A.D. 79, Mount Vesuvius, a nearby volcano, erupted violently. The eruption was so sudden that not everyone had a chance to flee the city. Many were either trapped in their houses and killed by hot ashes, or breathed poisonous gases and died trying to flee the city.

3   For about one hundred years following the 1748 rediscovery, excavations focused on uncovering the main buildings in Pompeii—the forum, the amphitheater, the theater, and the ornate houses. Then, in 1860, Giuseppe Fiorelli undertook a systematic block-by-block excavation of the city. Archeologists working at Pompeii in the 1900s decided that they should leave what they found intact and try to restore buildings to their original condition.

4   So far, about 75 percent of the city has been excavated. People who visit the site today can stroll along the streets and visit the homes and buildings of the ancient town. Thanks to the discovery of Pompeii, we have learned a great deal about the ancient Romans and their customs.

---

27 What is the main idea of this passage?

  A The uncovering of Pompeii was a vital historical discovery.

  B Many people perished in the eruption of Vesuvius.

  C The city of Pompeii remained hidden for 1,700 years.

  D Giuseppe Fiorelli excavated the city block by block.

28 When was the methodical excavation begun?

  A A.D. 79

  B 1748

  C 1860

  D the 1900s

GO ON ▷

29 Which detail supports the main idea that the uncovering of Pompeii was a vital historical discovery?

   A Pompeii has taught us a great deal about the ancient Romans and their customs.

   B In A.D. 79, a nearby volcano named Mount Vesuvius erupted violently.

   C A peasant digging in a vineyard unearthed a section of buried wall in 1748.

   D About 75 percent of the city has been excavated so far.

30 What is the author's view of the importance of the discovery of Pompeii? Cite two details from the passage to support your answer. (3 points)

_____

_____

_____

_____

_____

_____

Directions: Read the passage and answer the questions that follow.

A Fascination with Disaster

A natural disaster is a catastrophe that has its origin in the natural world. Hurricanes, tsunamis, floods, tornadoes, and volcanic explosions are a few examples. Natural disasters have always been with us, from as far back in undocumented history right up to the present time. Humans, it seems, are fascinated by natural disaster. Some of them can even render the vilest, most tragic disaster poetic with the turn of a phrase.

When Vesuvius erupted and showered Pompeii with volcanic ash and pumice, the cloud of falling debris blocked out the light of the sun. Although we have no firsthand accounts of the disaster written by the volcano's victims in Pompeii, we do have a firsthand account written by Pliny the Younger. This man watched the disaster unfold from a secure spot across the Bay of Naples. Pliny the Younger wrote, "Darkness fell, not the dark of a moonless or cloudy night, but as if the lamp had been put out in a dark room."

If Pliny the Younger were alive today, he would no doubt be fascinated to read about the archeological excavations of Pompeii that have been carried out since the mid-18th century. According to some scholars, approximately two thirds of Pompeii has been excavated, revealing many of the disaster's secrets to modern scholars and students.

31 How does the writer use a primary source to help explain a key idea about natural disasters? Use examples from the passage to support your answer. (3 points)

_____

_____

_____

_____

_____

_____

_____

_____

_____

_____

_____

_____

_____

Directions: Use both "Pompeii and Vesuvius" and "A Fascination with Disaster" to answer the following question.

32 The authors of "Pompeii and Vesuvius" and "A Fascination with Disaster" give conflicting information about—

   A when Vesuvius erupted.

   B how much of Pompeii has been excavated.

   C when a peasant discovered a wall of Pompeii.

   D whether Pliny the Younger was a survivor of the disaster.

GO ON ⇨

The Meyers Independent

LETTERS TO THE EDITOR   MARCH 5

Down with DST!

1   Citizens Against Daylight Saving Time is a group of concerned individuals that is trying to put a stop to the ridiculous practice of Daylight Saving Time. We are holding a meeting on March 10 in the auditorium of Meyers High School to organize our efforts.

2   Daylight Saving Time is a waste of precious time. When Benjamin Franklin came up with the idea for Daylight Saving Time back in the 1700s, he probably had only one watch or clock to turn ahead and move back. It takes me almost an hour to adjust the many clocks in our home. Some people also have to reprogram their electronic equipment and microwaves and adjust the clocks in their cars.

3   Even more important, however, is the effect Daylight Saving Time has on our bodies. Our bodies have a difficult time adjusting to an hour difference twice a year. A study done in 2007 found that when people move their clocks ahead in the spring, their bodies' internal rhythms don't adjust properly. We wind up hungry before mealtimes and tired before bedtime. The time change makes it difficult to fall asleep at night and disrupts normal sleeping patterns. It takes many people over a week to completely adjust to the change. In the interim, they are extremely <u>disoriented</u>. Ordinary tasks like driving an automobile become difficult and dangerous. Furthermore, too little sleep makes us more likely to catch colds and other illnesses. Daylight Saving Time makes you sick! The extra hour of daylight is much more trouble than it's worth.

4   Lastly, there is no longer a need for Daylight Saving Time. The energy saved by this program is little, and our country is no longer facing an energy crisis. Americans must stick together and demand that this unnecessary practice be stopped.

5   Citizens Against Daylight Saving Time is holding a meeting in the auditorium of Meyers High School on March 10. Senator Sydney Silverman will be present at the meeting. Senator Silverman knows that getting rid of Daylight Saving Time is the right thing to do! All intelligent citizens of Meyers will be present on March 10 to begin our fight to put an end to this ridiculous, outdated practice. Be there!

Mark Harrison
1541 Main Street

33 Which statement from the passage is a fact that supports the author's argument that DST should be ended?

  A *The time change . . . disrupts normal sleeping patterns.*

  B *The extra hour of daylight is much more trouble than it's worth.*

  C *. . . there is no longer a need for Daylight Saving Time.*

  D *A study done in 2007 found that when people move their clocks ahead in the spring, their bodies' internal rhythms don't adjust properly.*

34 Which statement from the passage is an example of loaded language?

  A *We are holding a meeting on March 10 . . . to organize our efforts.*

  B *Daylight Saving Time is a waste of precious time.*

  C *Some people also have to reprogram their electronic equipment and microwaves . . .*

  D *Senator Sydney Silverman will be present at the meeting.*

35 Which of the following is the author's response to the viewpoint that Daylight Saving Time is needed to save energy.

  A Daylight Saving Time is outdated.

  B It takes too long to set the clocks back.

  C Americans must stand together to end Daylight Saving Time.

  D We aren't facing an energy crisis so we don't need Daylight Saving Time.

36 In paragraph 3, the writer claims that Daylight Saving Time makes people sick. Evaluate the author's reasoning. Does he present any evidence to support this claim? Identify any irrelevant evidence. (5 points)

_____

_____

_____

_____

_____

_____

_____

_____

Take a break. Then go on to Part 3.

Directions: Read the following questions. Then choose the best answer.

37 Read the following sentence.

Her favorite hobby is <u>skateboarding</u>.

The underlined word is a(n)—

A gerund.

B participle.

C verb.

D infinitive.

38 Read the following sentence.

I want <u>to learn</u> Spanish before my trip to Mexico.

The underlined words are a(n)—

A gerund.

B participle.

C prepositional phrase.

D infinitive.

39 Which of the following sentences is written in **passive** voice?

A I ate the apple for dessert.

B She will be staying with us over the holidays.

C The e-mail was written by my teacher.

D I sent a reply before I proofread it.

40 Which of the following is an **interrogative** sentence?

A Schools of tropical fish swam past us.

B Did you see the fish with yellow spots?

C Oh! There's a huge blue fish!

D Be sure you draw each fish you see.

41 Which of the following is an **imperative** sentence?

A Walk your dog everyday.

B Cats are so much smarter than dogs!

C Do you have any pets?

D If I see your dog, I will tell you.

42 Which of the following sentences does NOT contain a shift in voice or mood?

   A Beat the eggs, and then you should add the salt.

   B I hit the ball, and the ball was caught by Sarahi.

   C If we want to go to the park, it's raining.

   D If we can't find the ball, then we can't play baseball.

43 Which sentence uses correct capitalization?

   A One of my favorite poems is "the Raven" by Edgar Allan Poe.

   B My friend prefers "The Bells," another poem by Poe.

   C Poe also wrote a short story titled "The pit And The Pendulum."

   D Edgar Allan Poe is one of America's foremost Poets.

44 Which sentence uses correct capitalization?

   A The Golden Gate bridge is a very long suspension bridge.

   B It connects San Francisco to Marin County, North of the city.

   C Another long suspension bridge is in the State of Michigan.

   D It spans the Straits of Mackinac in the northern part of the state.

45 Which sentence punctuates dialogue correctly?

   A Marcy asked "Who will come with me?"

   B "If you can wait five minutes," said Ted, "I'll be able to come."

   C "Thanks, said Marcy I'd appreciate your help."

   D "I'm always happy to be of assistance" said Ted with a laugh.

46 Which of the following sentences does NOT contain correct punctuation?

   A Let me think. . . . No, I don't know the answer.

   B My goal is to finish—and I do mean *finish*—my paper tonight.

   C John Adams—the second president of the United States—was the first president to live in the White House.

   D Steve Jobs, who died in October of 2011, was the mastermind behind the iPhone and iPad.

47 Which sentence is punctuated correctly?

   A Until he went to Europe last summer; Marco had never been out of this country.

   B He visited England, Spain France, and Portugal.

   C Marco liked Spain the best, he liked Portugal the least.

   D When he returned, he gave me three souvenirs: a T-shirt, a calendar, and a book.

48 Which sentence does NOT include misspelled words?

    A The quarry near my house would make a fantastic swimming hole.

    B Unfortunately, no swimming is allowed on the premeses.

    C The sheer rock walls and deep water make it a perilus place to swim.

    D As a result, we all go to the communitty pool to swim instead.

49 Which sentence does NOT include misspelled words?

    A Wanda has had perfect attendence for the passed three years.

    B She received an award at an assembly last week.

    C The principal congratulated her on her acheivement.

    D Wanda said she inntends to continue to make it to school every day.

50 Rewrite the following sentence so that it is in active voice. (1 point)

The ambassador was sent by the President on a diplomatic mission to Sudan.

_____

_____

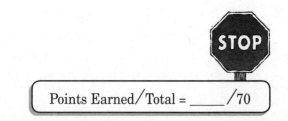

Points Earned / Total = _____ /70

Reading Literature Lesson 1

Cite, Infer, and Summarize

Review the Standards (RL.8.1, RL.8.2, W.8.9)
- Cite **evidence** from a text
- Draw **inferences** from a text
- **Summarize** the text

Q: What is **evidence**?

A: When answering questions or writing about a text, you must cite, or give, **evidence** to support your answer. Evidence includes details or direct quotations from the text. **Example:** Because the king says, "I can't risk losing my kingdom," we can conclude that he is motivated by a desire to stay in power and not by love for his people.

Q: How do I draw an **inference**?

A: An **inference** is a reasonable guess. To draw an inference, you combine clues from the text and information already know. For example, if a character breaks out in a cold sweat whenever he gets near a dog, you can infer that the character is afraid of dogs.

Q: How do I **summarize** a story?

A: A **summary** of a story should include the setting, the main characters, and the major events explained in chronological order. Do not include minor characters, minor events, or your opinions.

➲ Try It

Directions: Read the passage. Then answer the questions that follow.

Ming's First Customer

Ming and her mother stepped out of the car, laughing about something they had heard on the radio. "I can't wait to start my own business," Ming said excitedly as she walked up the creaking steps to the house. She looked around. The porch was overgrown with lilac bushes, and the windows were covered in cobwebs. Suddenly, a cloud covered the sun, and the day grew dark. A cool breeze made Ming shiver.

"I don't know whether I can knock on the door," Ming told her mother. "They don't look like the kind of people who want their lawn mowed."

"Oh, honey," Ming's mother said, "I saw Mr. Daley at the grocery store just the other day, and he told me that he needed some extra help."

Ming's hands felt clammy as she rang the doorbell. She thought she heard a cat howling inside the house. Then, she listened to the ominous sound of footsteps inching their way towards the front door. She began to doubt whether she really wanted to start a

GO ON →

lawn-mowing business, even though she loved working outside and was looking forward to buying a mountain bike with all of the money she would earn. As the door creaked open, Ming held her breath.

"Yes," growled a voice.

"Hi, I'm . . ." Ming started to stutter. "Hi. I mean . . ."

The door opened wider, and a man with a long white beard stood in the doorway.

"What is your business?" the man said.

"Hi, I'm . . ." Ming was still having trouble speaking.

"Cat got your tongue?" the man asked just as a yellow cat snaked out the door. "Lucy!" the man cried after the cat. "Don't let her escape," he said to Ming.

Suddenly Ming sprang to action, and chased the cat into a corner of the porch and scooped her up.

"Here's your cat, Mr. Daley," Ming said, putting the cat in the man's shaking hands. "I'm Ming, and my mother said you might need some help with yard work."

"Thank you," Mr. Daley said. "I can see that you're very good with your hands. You're just the person to help me get my yard back to shape."

After Ming and Mr. Daley had discussed what needed to be done first, Ming and her mother walked back down the stairs. Now, instead of seeing cobwebs and overgrown bushes and a yard full of weeds, Ming thought about how much better the porch and yard would look after a little hard work.

"See," Ming's mother said, "that wasn't so bad after all."

The sun reappeared, and Ming smiled, thinking about what a beautiful day it was.

---

1 All of the following could be used as evidence to support the idea that Mr. Daley needs help EXCEPT?

   A Mr. Daley's porch was overgrown with lilac bushes.

   B Ming told her mother, "they don't look like the kind of people who want their lawn mowed."

   C Ming's mother says that Mr. Daley told her he needed some extra help.

   D The windows were covered in cobwebs.

2 We can infer that Mr. Daley's attitude toward Ming changes because—

   A Ming helps him with his cat.

   B Ming's mother convinces him that Ming will do a good job.

   C Ming tells him about wanting to buy a mountain bike.

   D Ming doesn't know what to say to him.

3 Write a summary of the story. Be sure to include the setting, characters, and main events. (3 points)

_____

_____

_____

_____

_____

_____

_____

_____

4 How does the description of the weather change from the beginning to the end of the story? What is the relationship between the weather and Ming's attitude?

_____

_____

_____

_____

_____

For **Example 1**, you must evaluate which **evidence** from the text supports the idea that Mr. Daley needs help. Evidence from the story includes the appearance of Mr. Daley's lawn and house (choices A and D) and what Ming's mother says about Mr. Daley (choice C). Choice B does not support the idea. **Choice B** is the correct answer.

Example 2 asks you to make an **inference** about why Mr. Daley's attitude changes. Eliminate choices B and C because these things do not happen in the story. Choice D does happen in the story, but it clearly doesn't change Mr. Daley's attitude toward Ming. Because Mr. Daley says, "I can see you are good with your hands" after Ming catches his cat, we can infer that this is why his attitude toward Ming changes. **Choice A** is correct.

For **Example 3**, you must write a summary of the story. Remember that a good summary of a story includes the setting, main characters, and main events.

Good: _Ming is starting a lawn-mowing business to earn money for a new mountain bike. Her mother tells her that Mr. Daley, an older neighbor, needs help. When she goes to talk to him, she is scared by his gruffness and can't speak. But then she helps capture Mr. Daley's cat, and Mr. Daley realizes that Ming would be a good person to help him._

This is a poor response because it leaves out key details from the passage.

Poor: _Ming goes to talk to Mr. Daley about mowing his lawn. He's kind of mean to her, but he lets her help with his lawn._

For **Example 4**, you must draw **evidence** from a text to support your analysis of the story. A good answer will rephrase the question, draw a conclusion, and include specific evidence to support your conclusion.

Good: *The writer uses the weather to mirror Ming's attitude toward talking to Mr. Daley. At the beginning of the story, Ming sees the cobwebs and the unmowed lawn and gets nervous about talking to Mr. Daley. The sun goes behind a cloud and a "cool breeze made Ming shiver." After Ming talks to Mr. Daley and rescues his cat, she realizes that he is a nice man who needs help. She can see what the yard will look like when it's taken care of. The sun reappears, and Ming is happy.*

◎ Try It On Your Own

Directions: Read the passage. Then answer the questions that follow.

Mr. Daley's Travails

www.photos.com

Every time Mr. Daley heard the doorbell ring, he felt his heart start to race. The journey from the couch where he liked to sit reading the newspaper seemed so long since his joints had tightened up. Sometimes by the time he reached the door, no one was there. He would wonder whom he had missed, and he would think sadly about how much he would have liked the company.

"Yes, Lucy," he said to his companion, a yellow tabby, "times have certainly changed. People used to linger, not rush. Used to have visitors all the time."

He was just beginning to read the garden section, his favorite, even though he could no longer get out into the yard as much as he liked, when the inevitable happened: the doorbell rang. Lucy began to howl, as though she thought the old man couldn't hear it.

"I know, Lucy, I know," he cried. "I'm going as fast as I can."

But fast he wasn't. It was so frustrating! He had to take small careful steps. If he rushed, he could catch his toe on the carpet and go tumbling over, and then things would be worse.

Lucy turned up the volume.

"I'm coming," Mr. Daley bellowed. "I'm coming."

When he finally reached the door, Lucy rubbed back and forth against his leg. He was out of breath. "Yes," he said, aware his voice didn't sound right.

The girl with black hair didn't say anything.

"What's your business?" he asked, because he couldn't think of anything else to say.

Then, Lucy—silly cat!—made her getaway. She loved being outside, but Mr. Daley didn't let her roam freely for fear that she would become stuck up in a tree, and he wouldn't be able to get her down. Luckily, the girl caught Lucy, and told him her name was Ming. She wanted to help care for his yard.

   The journey back to the couch was still long, but Mr. Daley felt light on his feet. He was looking forward to sitting on his front porch, telling Ming what to do to make his yard look beautiful again. He was looking forward to the company! Maybe he would even let Lucy outside as well.

5   How does Lucy the cat influence the action of the story? Cite evidence from the text to support your answer. (3 points)

_____

_____

_____

_____

_____

_____

_____

_____

_____

_____

_____

6   Based upon the passage, we can infer that—

   A Mr. Daley doesn't like children or animals.
   B doesn't care about his lawn or his house.
   C is a lonely man.
   D is going to die soon.

7   Which of the following details should be included in a good summary of the story?

   A Mr. Daley likes to read the garden section of the paper.
   B The doorbell rang, but it took Mr. Daley a long time to get to the door.
   C Lucy rubbed back and forth against his leg.
   D Mr. Daley used to have visitors all the time.

Character and Theme

Review the Standards (RL.8.2, RL.8.3, RL.8.9)

- Determine how a **theme** is developed through the **characters**, **setting**, and **plot**
- Analyze how **dialogue** or incidents propel the action, reveal character, or provoke a decision
- Analyze how a modern work of fiction draws on themes, patterns of events, or character types from myths, traditional stories, or religious works

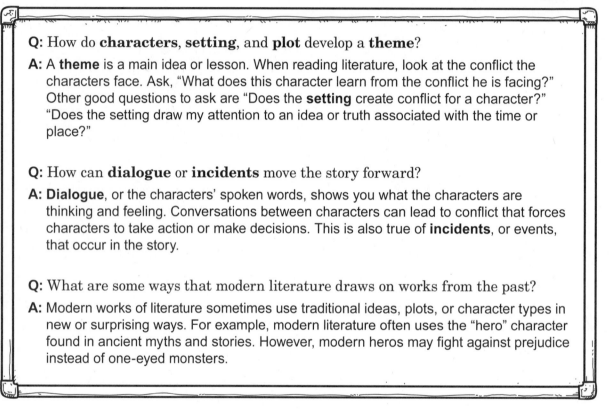

Q: How do **characters**, **setting**, and **plot** develop a **theme**?

A: A **theme** is a main idea or lesson. When reading literature, look at the conflict the characters face. Ask, "What does this character learn from the conflict he is facing?" Other good questions to ask are "Does the **setting** create conflict for a character?" "Does the setting draw my attention to an idea or truth associated with the time or place?"

Q: How can **dialogue** or **incidents** move the story forward?

A: **Dialogue**, or the characters' spoken words, shows you what the characters are thinking and feeling. Conversations between characters can lead to conflict that forces characters to take action or make decisions. This is also true of **incidents**, or events, that occur in the story.

Q: What are some ways that modern literature draws on works from the past?

A: Modern works of literature sometimes use traditional ideas, plots, or character types in new or surprising ways. For example, modern literature often uses the "hero" character found in ancient myths and stories. However, modern heros may fight against prejudice instead of one-eyed monsters.

⮕ Try It

Directions: Read the passage. Then answer the questions that follow.

The Ballet Musician

Olivia opened the studio door with a feeling of dread. Her parents encouraged her to take ballet, believing that it would help her become more graceful and refined. Unfortunately, Olivia was naturally clumsy, and ballet was an absolute nightmare. She hung her head and frowned as she climbed the studio's stairs.

Olivia remembered last week's class, when all the students took turns spinning and jumping across the floor. Mademoiselle Martine seemed to enjoy pointing out the flaws in her performance that day.

"Keep your chin up, Olivia," she said. "Stay on your toes."

Olivia had tried her best, but coordination simply seemed to elude her. At the end of class, Mademoiselle Martine had invited Olivia to come to this week's class early so the two could work together privately.

Today, Olivia arrived at the studio an hour before the start of class. As she set down her bag, she noticed a piano in the corner of the studio for the first time. Olivia sat down and began to play a song she learned last year. When she finished playing, she saw Mademoiselle Martine watching from the doorway. She told Olivia that her piano-playing sounded lovely. Then she stared for a minute and asked, "Olivia, do you enjoy ballet?"

Olivia hesitated. She thought she should be honest. "I might enjoy it if I wasn't so terrible at it," she said. "I've never been very coordinated. And I'm terrified of performing at the dance recital next month."

"I have an idea," Mademoiselle Martine said with a smile. "Since you obviously like playing the piano, and you sounded quite good to me, would you like to play at the recital instead of dancing?" Olivia's huge grin told Mademoiselle Martine that the answer was a definite yes.

---

1 What is the theme of this story?

A Practice makes perfect.

B Some people should not try to be dancers.

C Adults always know best.

D Sometimes a person's true talent can be hidden.

2 Which traditional character is Olivia MOST like?

A Romeo, who fell in love with a forbidden girl

B the ugly duckling, who discovered his true beauty

C Prometheus, who stole fire from the god Zeus and gave it to humans

D the puppet named Pinocchio, who wanted to become a real boy

3 How does Olivia's decision to be honest with Mademoiselle Martine help Olivia solve her problem with dancing?

_____

_____

_____

_____

In **Example 1**, you must identify the **theme** of the story. To identify a theme, you need to think about the **characters**, **setting**, and **plot** of the story.

Character: Olivia struggles with ballet but enjoys playing the piano.

Setting: The story takes place in a dance studio, a place that fills Olivia with dread.

Plot: Olivia tries without success to become a good dancer. While playing the piano, an activity she both enjoys and excels at, she reveals her true talent.

You can determine that the best answer is **Choice D.**

Example 2 asks you to compare Olivia, a character in a modern story, to characters in traditional stories to determine which character she is most like. Olivia does not fall in love or bestow a gift on anyone, so you can eliminate Choices A and C. She is already a real girl, so she is not like Pinocchio. She does discover her true talent after feeling like a failure, much like the ugly duckling discovered his true beauty. **Choice B** is correct.

For **Example 3**, you must think about how **dialogue** from the story helps move the plot forward. A good response includes specific details from the passage to support your answer.

Good: _When Mademoiselle Martine asks Olivia if she truly enjoys ballet, Olivia must decide whether to admit that she really doesn't enjoy dancing. She decides to be honest, and she tells her teacher that she feels untalented, uncoordinated, and terrified about dancing. This conversation moves the plot forward because the teacher responds by asking Olivia to play the piano instead of dancing at the recital. Olivia feels relieved and happy, and her problem with dancing is solved._

This is a poor response because it doesn't tell how the dialogue moves the plot forward to the solution of Olivia's problem.

Poor: _Olivia has a problem. She doesn't like dancing, and she dreads going to class. She does not really want to dance in the recital. She finally tells Mademoiselle how she feels._

Directions: Read the passage. Then answer the questions that follow.

Jacob and the Etosha Rhinos

Jacob eagerly climbed into the park ranger's Jeep. He was headed out to see rare black rhinos in Etosha National Park. His father's job had brought them to the African country of Namibia for the summer. Mr. Millerton was assisting the Namibian government with a project aimed at preserving the few black rhinos left in the park. Now, as they headed toward Etosha with Joseph Masunga, Jacob was glad that his father had asked him to come to Namibia. What a thrill it would be to see a real rhinoceros in the wild! And he'd have the best stories to tell his classmates when he returned to school in the fall.

As they drove, Joseph told them about the park.

"Etosha was established as a national wildlife sanctuary in 1967," he said with obvious pride. "It is one of the few places in southern Africa where you will find the endangered black rhino."

"Why are they endangered?" Jacob asked, having a hard time imagining the animals disappearing.

Joseph sighed and gazed out at the dusty landscape. "Greedy people kill black rhinos for their horns. They sell them for considerable sums of money." His voice rose with emotion as he spoke. "In some parks the poachers have wiped out all but one or two black rhinos."

"Yes, I have heard that armed guards must follow them to ensure that they are not slaughtered," Jacob's father added.

Joseph nodded. "Thankfully we have not had to do that here—yet," he said, turning into the park. He parked the vehicle under a grove of trees overlooking a water hole. At dusk they caught their first glimpse of a black rhino.

"A female and a calf," Joseph whispered.

Jacob was in awe. "She's huge!" he exclaimed, peering through his father's binoculars. The creature was so proud Jacob couldn't understand how anyone could kill it.

"Yes, a full-grown female black rhino can weigh more than a ton," Joseph said. "Notice how she walks behind her calf. That's how she protects it from predators who might sneak up from behind."

"Why don't the rhinos just run away from poachers?" Jacob asked.

"They do," the ranger replied. "But the poachers use big guns and trucks, so the rhinos don't stand a chance of getting away."

©Corel

For the next few moments in the silence of the vast landscape, Jacob enjoyed watching the pair drink and bathe in the water hole. He thought to himself that they looked more like moving rocks than animals. On the baby's long snout, he could see the nub of a horn. He couldn't imagine any amount of money that would justify the deaths of these one-of-a-kind creatures.

Suddenly the sound of a motor broke the quiet. Jacob turned his binoculars and saw a vehicle kicking up a thick cloud of dust.

"Poachers!" Joseph said.

The truck pulled up about fifty yards away, and Jacob could see two men with large guns start to get out. A third man emerged. He was carrying a saw.

"Get down!" the ranger ordered as he started the Jeep. Both Jacob and his father dropped to the floor.

Suddenly Jacob heard shouting. "They've spotted us!" Joseph said, stomping on the accelerator. The Jeep lurched into movement, bouncing Jacob back and forth as it soared over the rough ground.

Three doors slammed in unison. A motor revved and tires spun as the other vehicle took off.

Jacob expected the chase to last, but as quickly as he had started, Joseph stopped the truck. He picked up the radio and alerted the other rangers in the park. "Poachers on the maintenance road heading south," he told them. Then he turned to his passengers. "You can get up now," he said.

"Why aren't you going after them?" Jacob asked, angered by the idea of them getting away.

"I don't have to," Joseph replied, smiling grimly. "There's only one way out of the park, and long before they reach it, two rangers will be waiting for them with the local constable, who just happens to be in the park today looking for ways to stop the poachers! We were lucky today, very lucky."

Joseph glanced back at the water hole. The mother rhino and her baby had disappeared. They were safe—at least for now.

Jacob thought about what had just happened. He was excited to tell his friends about his adventure, but he was even more moved to do something about it. He decided that he would learn more about the Etosha rhinos and try to convince others to help save them from extinction.

---

4 How does Jacob change his view of the black rhinos from the beginning of the story to the end? Describe how the actions and words of other characters inspired the change in Jacob. Use at least two details from the passage to support your answer. (3 points)

_____

_____

_____

_____

_____

_____

_____

5 What is the theme of this story?

   A making friends

   B obeying adults

   C respecting animals

   D unexpected kindness

6 How does the author use action to show that the rhinos are truly endangered?

   A by having Joseph drive Jacob and his father to the water hole

   B by having Joseph explain why the rhinos are vulnerable

   C by having Jacob see a mother rhino and her baby

   D by having the poachers arrive with a saw and guns

7 Jacob wants to protect the mighty yet endangered rhinos. He is MOST like—

   A a boy in a Native American tale who tries to convince white people to stop slaughtering the buffalo.

   B a fox who cannot reach the grapes high on the vine and declares, "The grapes were sour anyway."

   C a boy who grows up among the apes of the jungle, thinking he is one of the animals.

   D a man who catches a magic fish that gives him three wishes if he will let the fish go free.

Test-Taking Tips

1 To cite evidence to support your answer, go back to the story and look for details, dialogue, or events that help make your answer clear or correct.

2 To draw inferences, look for details in the passage to support your answer. Combine the clues with your own knowledge and experience to figure out the correct answer.

3 Questions about a work's theme are asking you about the work's main idea or lesson. Think about the problem or conflict in the story and how the main character solves it. Think about what the main character learns from the conflict.

4 To analyze how a modern work uses themes, patterns of events, or character types found in traditional literature, ask yourself questions such as the following: *Do these stories teach a similar lesson? Do these characters face a similar problem or challenge? What personality traits do these characters share?*

Go for it!

Unit One Practice Test

Estimated time: 20 minutes

Directions: Read the following passage. Then answer the questions that follow.

Patricia's Decision

1   Patricia crept cautiously through the tangle of trees and bushes. A few feet before reaching a particularly dense thicket, she stopped and peered into its shadowy center. Her vision had been accurate. There in the grayness, curled in a tight ball, lay a tiny fawn.

2   "We should back off, Patty," her older brother Jonathan whispered. Patricia nodded and slowly swiveled around, trying to be as quiet as possible. Jonathan motioned for Patricia to follow. "The mother is probably foraging nearby. The longer we remain here, the longer the fawn will have to wait for her to return."

3   Patricia followed her brother back out through the trees, taking deliberate steps to avoid disturbing the fawn. When they reached a clearing, Patricia grabbed her brother's arm.

4   "What if that fawn was abandoned?" she said in a low tone. "We have to do something about it."

5   "That fawn wasn't crying, and it wasn't wounded," Jonathan said. "Most likely, its mother has already led it away from the thicket by now, and the best thing for that fawn is to be with its mother."

6   As the trail wound through the woods and led them back to their house, Patricia's thoughts remained in the thicket where she had seen the fawn. She had encountered numerous deer since they had moved to the piney woods of East Texas, but no solitary fawns. She was worried, and wanted desperately to help the young deer. Jonathan could tell from Patricia's silence that his sister was still preoccupied with their discovery.

7   "Look, it's still early," Jonathan said. "Let's check back later this afternoon, and if the fawn is still there, we can do something about it. But not until then, okay?"

8   Patricia brightened, thankful that her brother understood. She hoped the fawn would still be there in the afternoon so they could take it home and perhaps even raise it! A few moments later the two strode into the kitchen and joined their parents at the breakfast table. Patricia lost no time in relating their adventure.

9   "If the fawn is still there this afternoon, we're going to bring it home," Patricia said empathetically. "It needs us if it doesn't have a mother."

10   "Patricia, that fawn needs to learn how to survive without us, not with us," her father replied. "Even wild fawns can be dangerous. I'll go there with you with a crate to carry it back home if it truly has been abandoned."

11   Patricia frowned as she felt her enthusiasm wane. She was certain her nurturing would help the fawn if her father would allow it. She thought

intensely all day about a way to convince her father to let her help the fawn. Eventually her father's voice carried up to her room, telling her to put on her boots and get ready.

12 Patricia attempted to be stealthy as she, Josh, and her father approached the thicket. This time she heard the fawn long before she saw it. The fawn was crying, and when Patricia was finally able to spy it in the dim light, she could see that it had fire ants on its face.

13 "You two stay here," her father cautioned. "We need to capture this fawn before the fire ants do any further damage." Her father put on a pair of thick gloves, pushed his way into the brushwood, brushed away the ants, and gently scooped the stunned fawn into the crate. He closed the top, and together the three headed back toward the house, carrying the distressed fawn.

14 "We're going to put the fawn in the garage, where it's dark and quiet," her father informed them. "We need to give it as much peace as possible. I'm going to call the animal rehabilitator."

15 Patricia sighed in disappointment. This was the first time she's had an opportunity to care for a needy animal, and she was required to stay as far away as possible! Still, Patricia understood her father's reasoning. Even though she wanted to get close to the deer, she knew the fawn wouldn't share her enjoyment. She waited in the kitchen while her dad called the rehabilitation center.

16 About 20 minutes later Patricia heard a truck pull into the driveway. She scrambled outside and saw a tall woman emerge from the truck.

17 "Hello, I'm Audrey," the woman said as she shook Patricia's hand. "I hear you and your brother found an abandoned fawn on the trail today."

18 "Yes, we did. I'm Patricia, and I found the deer in a thicket behind the house this morning. Is there anything else we can do for it? I really want to help."

19 "What you did today was perfect. The best thing you can do for a deer that really is abandoned is to call a rehabilitation center," Audrey explained.

20 "Is there any way for me to come and visit it or be there with you when you release it?" Patricia asked. "I would volunteer some time if I could be close to the fawn."

21 Audrey grinned. "We always need volunteers in the center, but not to play with the deer. Mostly, people help us by answering the phones and maintaining our enclosures. I can't stress enough how important it is that the deer not become comfortable with people. In the wild, that could prove extremely dangerous."

22 Patricia contemplated Audrey's words as she watched her enter the garage and collect the fawn. She mulled over her options, wanting to put forth the best effort she could to help the deer return to the wild. Finally, she made a commitment to do what was best for the deer, even if it wasn't what was best for her.

1   On the lines below, write a summary of "Patricia's Decision." Include the setting, the main characters, and the main events. (3 points)

_____

_____

_____

_____

_____

_____

_____

_____

2   Which sentence from the story shows that Patricia agrees with her father's decision to contact the animal rehabilitator?

A *Patricia frowned as she felt her enthusiasm wane.*

B *Patricia brightened, thankful her brother understood.*

C *She waited in the kitchen while her dad called the rehabilitation center.*

D *Still, Patricia understood her father's reasoning.*

3   Based on Patricia's actions in the story, you can infer that she—

A cares about the best interests of animals.

B is too independent.

C is not reasonable even after hearing the facts.

D likes to argue.

4   The fawn in this story can be compared to which character type from traditional literature?

A the tricky coyote

B a lost sheep

C the wise owl

D the sly fox

5   Which best expresses the theme of the selection?

A Pets are fun to have.

B Volunteering is a good way to give to the community.

C Doing what's best is more important than doing what you want.

D Wild deer are frightening creatures.

6 Which detail from the passage supports the idea that Audrey is a trustworthy person with whom to leave the fawn?

   A Audrey emphasizes that the fawn should not become used to humans.

   B Audrey is a tall woman who drives a truck.

   C Audrey politely introduces herself to Patricia, Jonathon, and their dad.

   D Audrey grins when she answers one of Patricia's questions.

7 What causes Patricia's dad to decide to bring the fawn home?

   A Jonathon tells him that the fawn was in distress.

   B Audrey advises him to bring the fawn home.

   C He wants to make Patricia happy.

   D Fire ants have attacked the fawn's face.

8 What does Patricia's dialogue with her father in paragraphs 9 and 10 reveal about her father's character? (3 points)

_____

_____

_____

_____

_____

_____

_____

_____

_____

_____

_____

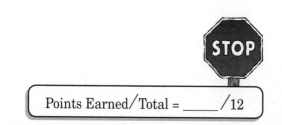

Points Earned/Total = _____/12

Reading Literature Lesson 3

Word Choice

Review the Standards (RL.8.4, L.8.5, L.8.5.a)

- Determine **figurative** and **connotative** meanings
- Analyze the impact of word choice, analogies, and allusions on tone and meaning

Q: What are **figurative** meanings?

A: Figurative language suggests something other than the literal meaning of the words. Examples of figurative language are similes, metaphors, and personification. To answer questions about figurative language, think about what ideas or emotions the author is trying to convey.

Q: What are **connotative** meanings?

A: A word's **connotation** is the feeling suggested beyond the word's exact meaning. For example, you can probably imagine a heavyweight boxer laughing, but can you imagine him giggling? The word *giggle* has childish, girlish, or immature connotations, but the word *laugh* does not.

Q: How does an author's word choice affect meaning and **tone**?

A: Writers choose their words carefully to communicate **tone**, or the writer's attitude or feeling toward the subject matter. You can also judge the tone of the writing based upon the analogies (comparisons) and allusions (references to other works) the writer uses. For example, if the writer compares his main character to a lost little lamb, the tone is sympathetic. You can usually describe a work's tone using adjectives, such as *formal, sarcastic, pessimistic, longing,* or *sad.*

➲ Try It

Directions: Read the passage. Then answer the questions that follow.

The Fish That Got Away

"What's the matter?" asked Sam's mother as Sam entered the back door with a mask of frustration on her face.

"That darn fish that I've tried to catch for months got away again. I'm at the end of my rope. I just know that Tom Reynolds is going to catch him, and I'll have to listen to him brag about it forever."

Sam and Tom, who lived on farms down the road from each other, had fished together since they were both six years old. Getting up at dawn on Saturday mornings, they would gather up their cane poles and bait, make sandwiches for their lunch, and head to the river that was <u>as slow as honey on a cold day</u>. Until a few months ago, they had always had a ball when they were together, but now it seemed their friendship was beginning to unravel just because of a fish. Tom had begun to boast that he would be the one to catch Buster, their name for the huge fish that always got away. From its sheer size, they assumed that Buster was a huge catfish. Some neighbors jokingly called the two friends Tom Sawyer and Huckleberry Finn.

Tom's bragging had made Sam all that more determined to catch Buster. She visualized the fish covered with corn bread batter, frying on the stove in her mom's black iron skillet.

The next morning when Sam got to the river, <u>the sun was a ghost in the sky</u>, and Tom was nowhere to be seen. Within five minutes of throwing her line in the water, Sam felt a tremendous tug. The fish pulled like a whale.

"Don't lose your cool," she kept telling herself.

When she felt the moment was just right, she yanked Buster to the shore. After what seemed to Sam a very long struggle, she got him into her fishing net. He was indeed a catfish, the king of catfish. His eyes looked as old as the earth, and when they caught hers, she knew what she must do. Sam removed the hook from Buster's mouth as though she were performing a delicate surgery. With a splash, Buster was once again in the water, and with a wave of his tail fin, he was gone.

Tom, who had been watching Sam and Buster, walked quietly to his usual spot on the riverbank. Without exchanging words, the two friends buried the hatchet. They had a long day of fishing in front of them.

www.photos.com

---

1 A river that is <u>as slow as honey on a cold day</u> is probably—

   A sweet.

   B fast-moving.

   C slow-moving.

   D the color brown.

2 The narrator says the <u>sun was a ghost in the sky</u>. This means that the sun was—

   A bright and hot.

   B barely visible.

   C eclipsed.

   D setting for the evening.

3 Which word or phrase from the passage is used to communicate a feeling of speed and strength?

   A *yanked*

   B *entered*

   C *gather up*

   D *removed*

GO ON

4 What do the neighbors mean when they compare Sam and Tom to Tom Sawyer and Huckleberry Finn?

   A that Sam and Tom seem to be imaginary people instead of real people

   B that Sam and Tom have traveled to the present from a time long ago

   C that Sam seems like a boy, even though she is a girl

   D that Sam and Tom are good friends who spend a lot of time together

5 What is the tone of the story? Give examples of how the author's word choice sets the tone of the story. (3 points)

_____

_____

_____

_____

_____

A **simile** is a kind of figurative language that compares two things that are not alike in order to describe something. Similes use the words *like* and *as* to compare two things. **Example 1** says that the river was *as slow as honey on a cold day*. To answer this question, you need to think about what cold honey is like and then what a river of cold honey would be like. The answer is **Choice C**, *slow-moving*.

Example 2 asks about **metaphor**, another kind of figurative language. A metaphor is a figure of speech that compares two unlike things by saying that one is another. In contrast to similes, metaphors do not use *like* or *as*. To answer this kind of question, you need to think about how the comparison enriches the meaning of the first item in the comparison. In this example, the author says the sun is a ghost. What do you think of when you imagine ghosts? They may be translucent or shadowy. The best answer is **Choice B** because ghosts may be *barely visible*.

To answer **Example 3**, you must think about the **connotations** of each answer choice. Each answer choice expresses an action, but only *yanked* has connotations of speed and strength. **Choice A** is correct. The other choices express actions that have connotations of unhurried movement.

Example 4 asks you to think about the meaning of the **allusion** to Tom Sawyer and Huckleberry Finn, characters created by the author Mark Twain. You may know that Tom and Huck spend a lot of time together having fun and having adventures. Based on this knowledge, you know that **Choice D** is correct. Even if you don't know anything about Tom and Huck, you can eliminate Choices A, B, and C because they do not make sense in the context of this story.

For **Example 5** you must identify and explain the **tone** of the story. A good response includes specific examples from the passage to support your answer.

Good: *The tone of the story is lively, showing the writer's genuine interest and pleasure in Sam's and Tom's dialogue and actions. Sam uses interesting figures of speech when she talks, such as "I'm at the end of my rope." Descriptive sentences use figures of speech and lively word choices such as "mask of frustration" and "unraveled" and "buried the hatchet."*

The tone reveals an attitude of lively interest in the characters, what they say, and what they do.

This is a poor response because it doesn't use examples from the story.

Poor: *The tone is the writer's feeling toward what he or she is writing about. You can look at words in the story to figure out the tone. This can be a challenge, like in the story about Sam and Tom.*

◎ Try It On Your Own

Directions: Read the following passage. Then answer the questions that follow.

This passage is a retelling of a story that is more than one thousand years old. The great warrior Beowulf defeated many monsters as a young man. Now he has been king for 50 years and must face a dragon that has attacked his people and burned their homes.

Beowulf and the Dragon

In his youth, Beowulf was as strong as an ox. He was old now, but because his spirit still burned brightly, he ordered a shield to be made of metal that could endure the dragon's flames. He gathered his bravest warriors and told them, "I, the king, alone will destroy this dragon and enrich our land with treasure."

When Beowulf called out his challenge, the dragon uncoiled itself and struck. Beowulf's shield melted like butter in the flames, and he could not reach the dragon to strike. Those chosen warriors became mice, scattering to the woods, leaving only one warrior, Wiglaf, who stood steady. "Cowards!" young Wiglaf yelled at the backs of the retreating men. "Our lord gave us the armor we stand in and the swords we carry when we feasted together in the hall. We pledged him our loyalty, and I for one will not return home a coward. Far better to perish in battle at my lord's side."

Wiglaf called to Beowulf, "Do this well, dear lord, as you have always done!" Under Wiglaf's shield, they waded through the dragon's choking fog. The dragon's fangs slashed Beowulf's neck just as the warrior struck his dagger, cutting short the monster's slaughter. At death's door, the king collapsed, poison conquering his body.

"Quickly," the king panted, "bring out the treasure, that I may see what I have won for my people before my life is an oft-told tale."

Wiglaf carried out the choicest treasures from the dragon's den; he gave Beowulf water to ease his pains. "I rejoice in this treasure," whispered Beowulf, "which with my life I have won for my people. If I had a son, I would now give it to him and give him rule of my people. Now you, Wiglaf, because you have not been a fair-weather friend and have dared to face the dragon, must take the throne."

One by one, the cowardly warriors emerged from their hiding places to gaze on their fallen king and the slain beast. Wiglaf, with tears on his face, reproached them angrily. "What will become of our people now? Our great king lies slain. Failing to defend your king is like giving the keys of the kingdom to your enemies as a gift. Our future is a book of tragedy."

6 The second paragraph says the <u>chosen warriors became mice</u>. This means that the warriors—

   A turned into mice.

   B became frightened.

   C shrank in size.

   D put on disguises.

7 What does the simile <u>Beowulf's shield melted like butter</u> mean?

   A Whatever the dragon touched turned into butter.

   B Beowulf was unprepared to meet the dragon.

   C The dragon's flames were extremely hot.

   D Beowulf's shield was made of butter.

8 The story ends with the sentence, "Our future is a book of tragedy." Based on events in the story, what does this metaphor mean? (3 points)

_____

_____

_____

_____

_____

9 Read the following sentence from the passage.

Failing to defend your king is like giving the keys of the kingdom to your enemies as a gift.

This analogy means that—

   A the cowardly warriors have doomed the kingdom.

   B Beowulf's warriors each carry a key to the kingdom.

   C the warriors have plotted with Beowulf's enemies.

   D the warriors should honor the tradition of giving gifts to enemies.

10 The writer uses words and phrases such as *perished, dear lord,* and *oft-told tale* to create a—

   A disrespectful tone.

   B sad tone.

   C humorous tone.

   D dignified tone.

Structure

Review the Standards (RL.8.5)

- Compare and contrast the **structure** of texts
- **Analyze** how the **structure** contributes to its meaning and style

Q: What is the **structure** of a text?

A: Structure refers to how a work is organized. The structure of a story refers to how the plot is arranged. You should consider the order of events including the rising action, climax, and denouement, or ending. The structure of poetry refers to how it is organized. Some poetry is structured with a pattern of rhyming lines in stanzas. Other poetry doesn't have a set pattern of rhyme or meter. A Venn diagram can help you compare and contrast the structures of two texts.

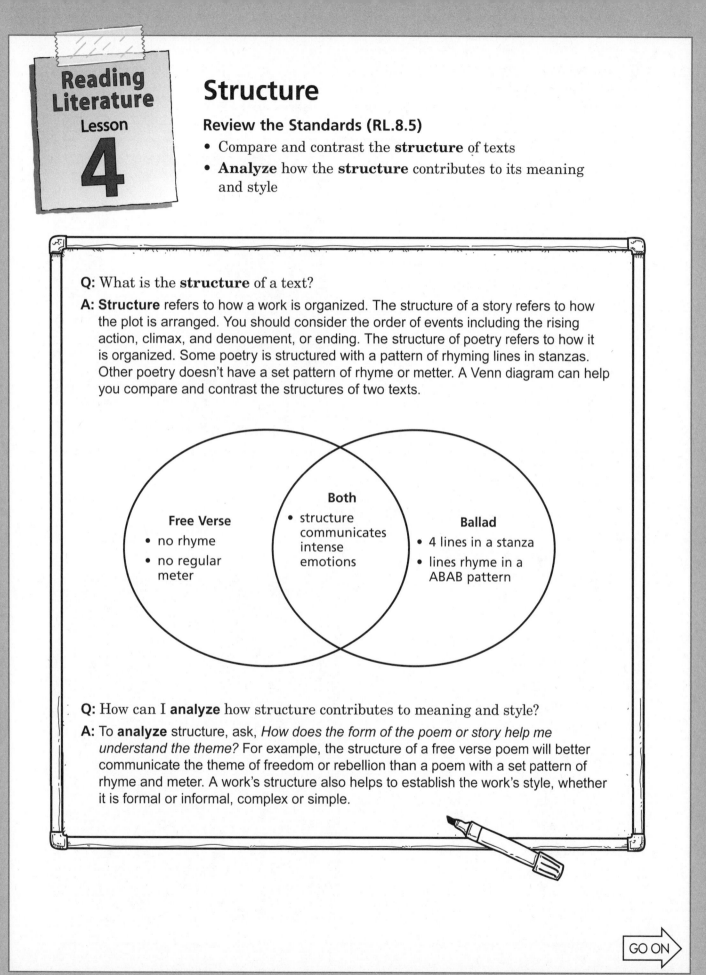

Both
- structure communicates intense emotions

Free Verse
- no rhyme
- no regular meter

Ballad
- 4 lines in a stanza
- lines rhyme in a ABAB pattern

Q: How can I **analyze** how structure contributes to meaning and style?

A: To **analyze** structure, ask, *How does the form of the poem or story help me understand the theme?* For example, the structure of a free verse poem will better communicate the theme of freedom or rebellion than a poem with a set pattern of rhyme and meter. A work's structure also helps to establish the work's style, whether it is formal or informal, complex or simple.

GO ON

Directions: Read the passages. Then answer the questions that follow.

The Eagle
(A Fragment)
by Alfred, Lord Tennyson

He clasps the crag with crooked hands;
Close to the sun in lonely lands,
Ringed with the azure world, he stands.

The wrinkled sea beneath him crawls:
He watches from his mountain walls,
And like a thunderbolt he falls.

www.Photos.com

A Red, Red Rose
by Robert Burns

O My Luve's like a red, red rose,
    That's newly sprung in June;
O My Luve's like the melodie
    That's sweetly played in tune.

5 As fair art thou, my bonnie lass,
    So deep in luve am I;
And I will luve thee still, my dear,
    Till a' the seas gang dry.

Till a' the seas gang dry, my dear,
10 And the rocks melt wi' the sun:
O I will love thee still, my dear,
    While the sands o' life shall run.

And fare thee weel, my only luve,
    And fare thee weel awhile!
15 And I will come again, my luve,
    Though it were ten thousand mile.

www.Photos.com

---

1   The short rhyming lines in "The Eagle (A Fragment)" create a—

   A complex, pessimistic style.

   B broken, confusing style.

   C simple, rhythmic style.

   D dreary, unhurried style.

2   In "A Red, Red Rose," each indented line—

   A rhymes with the line before it.

   B is an entirely new idea.

   C begins a new stanza.

   D explains the thought in the line before it.

3   Compare and contrast the structures of "The Eagle (A Fragment)" and "A Red, Red Rose." Use examples from BOTH passages to support your answer. (3 points)

_____

_____

_____

_____

   Example 1 asks you to think about the connection between the poem's **structure** and style. The short lines cause the poem to move along quickly rather than slowly, so you can eliminate Choice D. Each line expresses a complete thought, so the style is not confusing; eliminate Choice B. The short lines are more simple than complex, so you can eliminate Choice A. **Choice C** is the correct answer.

   To answer **Example 2**, you must think about the connection between the poem's **structure** and meaning. No indented line rhymes with the line before it, so Choice A is incorrect. The indented lines do not begin new stanzas, so eliminate Choice C. Each indented line builds on the thought in the line before it. **Choice B** is correct.

   For **Example 3** you must compare and contrast the structures of the two poems. A good response includes specific examples from both poems to support your answer.

   Good: _Both "The Eagle (A Fragment)" and "A Red, Red Rose" are arranged in fairly short lines of verse. However, the poems' stanza lengths are different. "Eagle" is set in two three-line stanzas. In contrast, "Rose" is set in four four-line stanzas. The poems use different rhyme schemes too. In "Eagle," all the lines in a stanza rhyme. For example, the lines in stanza one end in_ hands, lands, _and_ stands. _In "Rose," the second and fourth lines of each stanza rhyme. For example, the rhyming words from lines two and four are_ June _and_ tune.

   This is a poor response because it doesn't use examples from the poems.

   Poor: _The two poems are "The Eagle (A Fragment)" and "A Red, Red Rose." They are different because they are written by different writers. They have different structures._

Directions: Read the passages. Then answer the questions that follow.

Rain
by Robert Louis Stevenson

The rain is raining all around,
    It falls on field and tree,
    It rains on the umbrellas here,
    And on the ships at sea.

from **The Song of Hiawatha**
by Henry Wadsworth Longfellow

1   Swift of foot was Hiawatha;
2   He could shoot an arrow from him,
3   And run forward with such fleetness,
4   That the arrow fell behind him!
5   Strong of arm was Hiawatha;
6   He could shoot ten arrows upward,
7   Shoot them with such strength and swiftness,
8   That the tenth had left the bow-string
9   Ere the first to earth had fallen!

4 Read the following line from "Hiawatha."

Swift of foot was Hiawatha

Which of the following lines has the same structure as the one above?

A *He could shoot an arrow from him,*
B *That the arrow fell behind him!*
C *Strong of arm was Hiawatha*
D *He could shoot ten arrow upward.*

5 In "Rain," the use of many one-syllable words suggests

A a complex rhyme scheme.
B a violent rainstorm.
C the tap-tap-tap of raindrops.
D a feeling of suspense.

6 Compare and contrast the structures of "Rain" and the excerpt from *The Song of Hiawatha*. Use examples from BOTH passages to support your answer. (3 points)

_____

_____

_____

_____

_____

_____

_____

_____

_____

_____

_____

_____

GO ON

Point of View

Review the Standards (RL.8.6)

- Analyze how differences in the **points of view** of the characters, audience, or reader create suspense or humor

Q: How do I analyze **points of view**?

A: A **point of view** is the perspective from which a character, reader, or audience member experiences the story. For example, one character may know something that another character doesn't know. In response, the reader may feel suspense about what will happen when the second character finds out. To analyze points of view, ask, *What does one character know that one or more other characters don't know?* or *What does the reader know that one or more characters in the story don't know? Dramatic irony* is when the reader knows something that the characters don't know.

➲ Try It

Directions: Read the passage. Then answer the questions that follow.

Spying on Friends

1   "What a bummer!" Juan thought to himself. He had broken his leg in a skiing accident last weekend. Now his leg was in a cast and he would have to stay at home for several weeks while it healed. Juan was especially disappointed that he would not be able to participate in the neighborhood soapbox derby race. He had entered every year since 1998.

2   Juan tossed aside a magazine and looked out the window. His neighbor Wendy was sitting outside on her front porch with some other girls from school. After talking for a while, Wendy opened the garage door. Juan could see a big pile covered with a burlap sack. Wendy flipped off the cover and showed the girls what was underneath. Juan couldn't tell exactly what it was, but it looked like a cart on wheels. Wendy shut the garage door, and Juan couldn't tell where they went next.

3   The following day, Juan was watching a movie when he heard several cars pull up outside. He opened his blinds and saw that the same girls were gathering at Wendy's house again. They took the cart from the garage and wheeled it around to the backyard. "Darn!" Juan thought. He couldn't see anything now. He paid his little brother a dollar to go find out what the girls were doing in the backyard.

4   A few minutes later, his brother came back with news. "They're building something," he said. "They have a bunch of wood, some metal, and I think I saw some wheels. When they saw me, they tried to hide what they were doing."

5   "Aha!" thought Juan. "They're planning to enter the derby race this year!" According to the rules of the race, no one was allowed to get help on the cart that he or she planned to enter. If the girls were building racers together, that meant they were cheating. Juan immediately picked up the phone to tell his friend Eric what he had seen. They agreed that the best thing to do was to catch the girls red-handed.

6   Juan's friends gathered at his house. The plan was to wait until Wendy and her friends went to the backyard. Then Eric, Scott, and Wes would quietly walk around to the backyard carrying Juan's camera. Eric would create a commotion and the girls would look in his direction. Then Scott would pop out with the camera and snap photos of their vehicle. Wes would read the list of rules to the girls so they would know they had been caught. Juan would watch from the window and radio to the guys via walkie-talkie if anything suspicious occurred.

7   A car pulled up in front of Wendy's house. "Good luck!" Juan said to his friends. He saw the boys creep around the backyard. Juan leaned forward and could feel the adrenaline pumping through his veins. He waited, and waited, and waited. Nothing seemed to be happening. A few minutes later he whispered into his walkie-talkie, "Eric? Can you hear me?"

8   Eric's voice came over loud and clear. "Juan, you have an overactive imagination. They weren't building a cart for the soapbox derby! They're building a new clubhouse for their secret club, which we were just invited to join. Catch you later, man."

1   The reader experiences the action from whose point of view?

   A the girls'

   B Juan's

   C Juan's brother's

   D Eric's

GO ON

2 What makes the ending of the story funny?

    A Eric's realization that the girls were not building a cart for the soapbox derby

    B the reader's realization that Juan is stuck inside his house for weeks until his leg heals

    C the contrast between what Juan suspected the girls were building and what they actually were building

    D the clues that Juan collects by observing and listening to reports from his brother and friends

3 In "Spying on Friends," how do the differences in characters' viewpoints create suspense for the reader? Use details from the story to support your answer. (3 points)

_____

_____

_____

_____

_____

To answer **Example 1**, you must analyze the **points of view** of the characters. The story is told from Juan's point of view. He knows what he can see from his window and what his brother and friends report to him. What he most wants to know is something that only the girls know, until the end of the story: What are the girls building? You can conclude that **Choice B** is correct.

Example 2 asks you to think about how differences in characters' points of view, or knowledge, can create humor. Eric's realization is important, but it does not create the humor. You can eliminate Choice A. The information in Choice B is revealed early in the story, so you can eliminate Choice B too. Similarly, Juan gathers clues throughout the story, not just at the end, so Choice D is incorrect. The humor comes from the contrast between Juan's dark suspicions and the innocent truth of what the girls were doing. **Choice C** is correct.

For **Example 3** you must think about how differences in characters' viewpoints can create suspense for the reader. A good response includes examples from the passage to support your answer.

Good: *The story is told from Juan's viewpoint. This means that the readers knows only what Juan knows. Whatever Juan is curious about, the reader is curious about. Juan spies on Wendy from his window, and he gathers clues and reports from his brother and friends. The clues suggest that the girls might be building a derby car, but Juan (and the reader) remains in suspense about the truth. The end is highly suspenseful as Juan waits and waits to hear Eric's final report. The reader, too, must wait and wait, and the suspense builds.*

This is a poor response because it doesn't use examples from the passage.

Poor: *The reader and each character can have the same or different viewpoints on what is happening. When one character knows something that the reader doesn't know, the reader feels suspense.*

Directions: Read the passages. Then answer the questions that follow.

Charlotte's Big Scare

1 It was 9:00 on Wednesday night, and Charlotte was still at school. The entire cast of the fall play, *Midnight at the Old Inn*, had stayed late to get notes from the director, Ms. Lin. Only two days of rehearsals remained before the show opened on Friday night.

2 "Charlotte, I need you to be a little more frightened when you hear the mysterious noises at the old inn," said Ms. Lin.

3 "But Ms. Lin," Charlotte responded, "how can I be frightened when I know it turns out to be the wind making all the weird noises?"

4 "That's why it's called acting, Charlotte. You must *act* frightened," Ms. Lin replied.

5 "I'll give it my best shot," Charlotte said. Ms. Lin gave each student a few more notes and then dismissed the actors.

6 The following day, Charlotte practiced acting scared. When her math teacher assigned the class homework, she wore her best frightened face. But the teacher said, "Charlotte, don't look so surprised. You must be accustomed to homework assignments by now."

7 When Charlotte practiced looking scared in the lunch line, the cafeteria worker said, "If you think it smells bad, young lady, you don't have to eat it." No one seemed to believe that Charlotte looked frightened. Even Charlotte's best friends in the play didn't believe her.

8 "You don't really look scared," Samantha said. "Just annoyed."

9 "I think you look confused," added Antonio.

10 "Well, we'll see what Ms. Lin thinks tonight at rehearsal," Charlotte scoffed as she stormed away.

11 That evening, the cast gathered in the auditorium for the final dress rehearsal. It was a rainy night, just as it was in the play *Midnight at the Old Inn*. Anastasia, the assistant director, nodded at Charlotte. "Good luck tonight," she said. Charlotte smiled, but inside she was worried that she still might not appear frightened enough to please Ms. Lin.

12 The rehearsal started out as usual. A few actors stumbled over their lines. Antonio entered late for an important scene. But in the middle of the show, the lights suddenly flickered off. The auditorium was in total darkness. "Turn the lights back on!" someone shouted. Then a door slammed and the sound of faint, eerie flute music drifted into the room from somewhere far away. "What's that?" someone called. The music continued for a moment and then faded away.

13 Without warning, the lights came back on. The actors were all crowded together on the stage, looking nervously at one another. "What was

GO ON →

that strange music?" Samantha asked. "No one is here at this hour."

14   Ms. Lin looked around. "I don't know," she said, "but we need to continue." The actors returned to their places, still looking a little worried. Charlotte's big scene was coming up. She entered the stage set with Antonio. They were supposed to be entering the old inn for the first time. As they walked in, the lights began to flicker. Charlotte felt her heart beating, and suddenly the door to the set fell over with a crash. Charlotte jumped.

15   "You look pretty scared now," Antonio whispered.

16   "That's because I am," Charlotte whispered back. "Why are these strange things happening?"

17   "Just keep going," he said, trying to encourage her. When Charlotte was supposed to hear the whistling wind played over the speakers, she heard a strange stomping sound from above, as though something was happening on the roof. She looked out into the audience, but she couldn't see Ms. Lin or anyone else out there. It felt as if she and Antonio were truly all alone at the old inn. Charlotte's voice wavered as she spoke her lines, and her hands shook nervously. Finally they got to the end of the scene. The lights came up, and Ms. Lin began applauding from the audience.

18   "Great job, Charlotte, I knew you could do it," she said.

19   "Do what?" Charlotte asked.

20   "Look frightened! I really believed you were scared this time," Ms. Lin replied.

21   "That's because I was," Charlotte said. "Why did the lights keep going out? And what were those strange noises?" The other actors nodded their heads, for they were as curious as Charlotte.

22   "I really don't know," Ms. Lin answered. "It must be a mystery." Just then Anastasia entered through the rear door of the auditorium. She was wearing a rain jacket and large boots, and she was carrying a flute. When she saw everyone staring at her, Anastasia waved.

23   "Good job," she called. "Charlotte, you were great! So scared! Just keep it up tomorrow night and you'll have a great show."

4   In "Charlotte's Big Scare," how does a difference in the characters' viewpoints create humor? Use examples from the story to support your answer. (3 points)

_____

_____

_____

_____

_____

_____

_____

5 Which sentence in the story shows that Anastasia was responsible for the strange events during rehearsal?

A *She was wearing a rain jacket and large boots, and she was carrying a flute.*

B *Anastasia, the assistant director, nodded at Charlotte.*

C *As they walked in, the lights began to flicker.*

D *When she saw everyone staring at her, Anastasia waved.*

6 Why are certain events in the final dress rehearsal suspenseful?

A Neither Charlotte nor the reader knows what Ms. Lin will think of Charlotte's acting.

B Neither Charlotte nor the reader knows what is causing the spooky sounds.

C None of Charlotte's castmates know whether she will be able to act frightened in the play.

D The reader does not know how the plot in Charlotte's play will end.

Test-Taking Tips

1 When trying to determine the meaning of figurative language, use context clues, or other words in the sentence, to help you understand the meaning.

2 For questions involving word connotations, think about what the word suggests beyond its exact meaning. Look at how the word is used in the sentence. Then ask yourself, *What feeling is the author trying to communicate to readers?*

3 Remember that a writer's choice of words can reveal the writer's attitude or feeling toward the subject matter—the tone of the work.

4 To interpret an analogy, think about the relationship between the two things being compared. Writers use analogies to make the first thing in the comparison clearer or more meaningful.

5 To analyze how a work's structure contributes to its meaning and style, ask, *How does the work's form reveal its theme or meaning?* Think about how the sentence structure, rhyme, and genre (type of literature) support the theme. Consider how smaller sections of the passage work together to create meaning.

Go for it!

Unit Two Practice Test

Estimated time: 20 minutes

Directions: Read each passage. Then answer the questions that follow.

---

from "Song of Myself"
by Walt Whitman

The runaway slave came to my house and stopt outside,
I heard his motions crackling the twigs of the woodpile,
Through the swung half-door of the kitchen I saw him limpsy and weak,
And went where he sat on a log and led him in and assured him,
And brought water and fill'd a tub for his sweated body and bruis'd feet,
And gave him a room that enter'd from my own, and gave him some coarse clean clothes,
And remember perfectly well his revolving eyes and his awkwardness,
And remember putting plasters on the galls of his neck and ankles;
He staid with me a week before he was recuperated and pass'd north,
I had him sit next me at table, my fire-lock lean'd in the corner.

---

from Narrative of the Life of Frederick Douglass, an American Slave
by Frederick Douglass

I was born in Tuckahoe, near Hillsborough, and about twelve miles from Easton, in Talbot county, Maryland. I have no accurate knowledge of my age, never having seen any authentic record containing it. By far the larger part of the slaves know as little of their ages as horses know of theirs, and it is the wish of most masters within my knowledge to keep their slaves thus ignorant. I do not remember to have ever met a slave who could tell of his birthday. They seldom come nearer to it than planting-time, harvest-time, cherry-time, spring-time, or fall-time. A want of information concerning my own was a source of unhappiness to me even during childhood. The white children could tell their ages. I could not tell why I ought to be deprived of the same privilege. I was not allowed to make any inquiries of my master concerning it. He deemed all such inquiries on the part of a slave improper and impertinent, and evidence of a restless spirit. The nearest estimate I can give makes me now between twenty-seven and twenty-eight years of age. I come to this, from hearing my master say, some time during 1835, I was about seventeen years old.

1   In "Song of Myself," words and phrases such as *assured, gave,* and *next me* set a tone of—

   A jealousy.

   B sympathy.

   C fear.

   D anxiety.

2   The long, unrhymed lines in "Song of Myself" are used to—

   A tell a narrative about an experience the author had.

   B create a musical and rhythmic style.

   C imitate the speech patterns of the runaway slave.

   D suggest that the author did not take the experience seriously.

3   Read this line from "Song of Myself."

I had him sit next me at table, my fire-lock lean'd in the corner.

The speaker's point of view in this line helps to—

   A lighten the mood with a funny expression.

   B create humor by contrasting dinner time and firearms.

   C create suspense about where the slave is going.

   D create suspense about the danger they are in.

4   Compare and contrast the structures of the excerpts from "Song of Myself" and *Narrative of the Life of Frederick Douglass*. Do the structures create the same or different styles? Use examples from BOTH passages to support your answer. (3 points)

_____

_____

_____

_____

_____

_____

_____

_____

_____

_____

GO ON

5 In *Narrative of the Life of Fredrick Douglass,* which word is used to communicate a feeling of unfairness?

   A improper

   B source

   C deprived

   D estimate

6 In *Narrative of the Life of Fredrick Douglass,* Douglass uses the analogy of horses and age to show that—

   A slaves were sometimes no better off than animals.

   B slaves felt a special connection to animals.

   C slaves had to work as hard as horses worked.

   D masters took pride in their slaves and their horses.

7 Which metaphor BEST fits Frederick Douglass?

   A He was the apple of his master's eye.

   B He was a prisoner whose chains were the color of his skin.

   C His mind was a smooth slate without a mark on it.

   D Every day was a holiday in the story of his life.

8 The clear, direct sentences that make up the paragraph from *Narrative of the Life of Fredrick Douglass* help to create—

   A a self-important style of writing.

   B a playful style of writing.

   C an informative style of writing.

   D poetic style of writing.

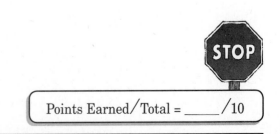

Points Earned/Total = _____/10

Reading Informational Text Lesson 6

Cite, Infer, and Summarize

Review the Standards (RI.8.1, RI.8.2, RH.8.1, RH.8.2, RST.8.1, RST.8.2, W.8.9)

- **Cite** the text
- Make an **inference**
- Determine a **central idea** of a text
- **Summarize** the text

Q: How do I **cite** the text?

A: When you analyze a passage, you need to give examples, details, or quotations from the work to support your ideas about the work. When you do this, you are **citing** the text.

Q: How do I make an **inference**?

A: An **inference** is an educated guess based on supporting evidence. For example, suppose a doctor tells you to wear sunscreen on your skin when you spend the afternoon at the lakeshore. Use details from what the doctor tells you along with your own knowledge to draw a conclusion.

Inference	Supporting Evidence
Exposure to the sun may be harmful to my skin.	• A doctor told me to wear sunscreen on my skin when I spend the afternoon at the lakeshore. • My doctor and I both know that people go to the lakeshore when it's sunny.

Q: How do I know what the **central idea** of a text is?

A: The **central idea** is the idea or argument that the passage is mainly about. Most works introduce the central idea in the first paragraph or the introductory section. Then each paragraph in the rest of the passage supports or develops the central idea.

Q: What should I include in a **summary**?

A: A **summary** of a passage should include the central idea, the main supporting details, and the conclusion. Do not include minor details or your opinions.

GO ON ➡

Directions: Read the passage. Then answer the questions that follow.

The Chinese discovered silk almost 5,000 years ago. Chinese legend credits the wife of Emperor Huangdi with the discovery. According to this story, the emperor was dismayed because the mulberry trees in his garden were being destroyed, and he ordered his wife to find out why.

She noticed that small white caterpillars were voraciously eating the leaves and spinning glistening cocoons. One day, while examining a cocoon, the empress accidentally dropped it into a pot of hot water. The spidery threads that surrounded the cocoon began to unwind into a single tiny glistening thread—silk. The empress found that when several fibers were gathered together, they formed a thick thread that could be woven into fabric.

The cloth woven from silk was featherlight, beautiful, and strong. When dyed, it acquired brilliant hues. The Chinese guarded the silk-making process vigilantly. For about 3,000 years, the Chinese alone knew the secret of the silkworm.

The Persians, who lived in what is present-day Iran, were among the first people outside China to see silk. Starting in about 200 B.C., Persian traders traveled to China to purchase silk, jade, and other precious goods. They then carried these treasures westward in camel caravans to Damascus, one of the ancient world's great marketplaces. There, other traders bought the silk and continued the return journey, eventually reaching the markets of the Roman Empire.

The trade route between China and Europe came to be known as the Silk Road. It was not a single route, but rather a complex, ever-changing network of camel paths and horse trails that traversed some of the world's highest mountains, hottest deserts, and most inhospitable landscapes. The entire route was about 5,000 miles long. It joined eastern China (what is now the city of Xi'an) with the Mediterranean Sea.

The majority of traders did not travel the entire length of the Silk Road; those traveling east and those traveling west met in the middle. The midpoint of the journey was Central Asia, in what is now the independent republic of Uzbekistan. The ancient cities of Bukhara and Samarkand were centers of commerce along the ancient Silk Road. There, traders met to exchange goods, rest, and buy supplies for the long journey home. Traders from the East brought silk, paper, spices, jade, and other goods the Western world prized but did not have the technology or resources to produce. Traders from Europe and the Middle East brought their own prized commodities, which included grapes, pomegranates, and Mediterranean colored glass.

For the traders, a journey along the Silk Road was long, arduous, and dangerous. The journey often took more than two years to complete. Travelers faced numerous dangers along the way. They had to cross vast scorching deserts and scale forbidding mountains without the aid of modern navigational tools, reliable maps, or roads. Bandits posed an ongoing threat to the caravans as well. Small towns and cities developed along the Silk Road. They offered travelers food, water, rest, and shelter, but there were often many miles between them.

By about 800 A.D., travel along the Silk Road started to decline. Sea routes had been established between China and Europe, and traders came to prefer the safer, less arduous journey by ship. In addition, Western cultures eventually learned the secrets of making silk and paper, so traveling to China's interior became unnecessary. By about the 14th century, traders no longer followed the Silk Road.

---

1   We can infer that the Silk Road was traveled by many people based upon which detail from the passage?

   A *Small towns and cities developed along the Silk Road.*
   B *The journey often took more than two years to complete.*
   C *Travelers faced numerous dangers along the way.*
   D *The entire route was about 5,000 miles long.*

2   Based on the information in this passage, you can tell that traders who traveled the Silk Road had—

   A maps and compasses.
   B stamina and courage.
   C large families.
   D formal training.

3   Which title **best** expresses the main idea of the passage?

   A The Empress and the Caterpillar
   B The Secret of Silk
   C Strong and Beautiful Silk
   D Save the Trees!

4   Which **best** summarizes the last paragraph of the selection?

   A By the 14th century, the Silk Road was no longer used. Traveling by sea was an easier and safer way to reach China. Also, Western cultures had learned how to make silk and paper themselves.
   B By about 800 A.D., sea routes had been established between China and Europe. Most traders traveled this way because it was safer and easier.
   C People in the western world learned the secrets of making silk and paper. This meant they no longer needed to get these things from China. As a result, the Silk Road was no longer used.
   D By about 800 A.D., travel started to decline along the Silk Road because sea routes had been established between China and Europe. Traders preferred to travel that way because it was safer and easier. Also, Western cultures learned how to make silk and paper. Traders didn't need to go to China to get these products. By the 14th century, the Silk Road was no longer used.

5 Based on information in the passage, what inference can be made about how silk was traded after the Silk Road was closed? Use at least two details from the passage to support your answer. (3 points)

_____

_____

_____

_____

_____

Example 1 asks you to **cite** the detail that supports the **inference** that the Silk Road was traveled by many traders. Choice B is a detail about the length of the journey, and Choice C is about dangers on the road. Choice D is about the length of the road. You can eliminate all three of these choices. You can infer that many travelers used the road based on the information that towns and cities developed along the road. **Choice A** is correct.

To answer **Example 2**, you must make an **inference**. The information in the passage focuses on how long the journey could take and the dangers of the journey. These details help you infer that travelers needed stamina and courage. **Choice B** is correct.

Example 3 tests your understanding of the **central idea**. Some test questions may ask you to choose a sentence from the passage that expresses the main idea or a statement that sums up the main idea. Other questions, like this one, ask you to choose the best title or an alternate title. The title of a passage should always reveal the central idea. The most important idea in the passage is that the Chinese discovered and kept secret the methods of making silk. The only title that expresses this idea is **Choice B**, _The Secret of Silk_.

Example 4 asks you to choose the best **summary** of one paragraph of the selection. A good summary includes the main idea or event and only the most important details. The last paragraph of the selection is about the decline of the Silk Road, so a good summary should include the details that tell why this happened. Choice A is the only summary that includes information about both reasons for the decline of the trade route. Choices B and C each include only one of the most important details. Choice D is not a summary because it simply restates all the information in the paragraph rather than giving only the most important ideas. **Choice A** is correct.

For **Example 5** you must make an inference about how silk was traded after the decline of the Silk Road. A good response includes at least two details from the passage to support your answer.

Good: _After the Silk Road closed down, silk was most likely traded using ships and sea routes. The passage states that sea routes between China and Europe were established by around 800 A.D., and merchants preferred these safer routes. Also, according to the passage, the secret of making silk became known to Western people, so they no longer had to travel all the way to the interior of China to get silk. There were people in their own country making silk._

This is a poor response because it doesn't make an inference about how silk was traded after the decline of the Silk Road. It simply gives details from the passage.

Poor: *The Silk Road closed down between 800 A.D. and the 14th century. This happened because traders were no longer using the Silk Road. They no longer needed to complete the dangerous, arduous, and long journey.*

◎ Try It On Your Own

6   The chart below lists two conclusions drawn from the passage. Complete the chart by writing details from the passage that support each conclusion. Include at least three details in total. (3 points)

Conclusion	Supporting Details
Emperor Huangdi's wife had a lively curiosity.	
Silk was a valuable product.	

7   What inferences can be drawn from the events that led to the decline of the Silk Road?

   A People have come to value silk less and less over time.
   B Resources are more important than technology.
   C Technological advances can change trade patterns.
   D The 14th century was a bad time for both artisans and traders.

8   Which sentence from the passage explains why silk was such a valuable product?

   A *The Chinese discovered silk almost 5,000 years ago.*
   B *The spidery threads that surrounded the cocoon began to unwind into a single tiny glistening thread—silk.*
   C *The cloth woven from silk was featherlight, beautiful, and strong.*
   D *The Chinese guarded the silk-making process vigilantly.*

GO ON ▷

9   Which of the following is the **best** summary of the information in the passage?

   A The Silk Road was a 5,000-mile trade route between China and Europe. Many important cities sprung up along the route, giving traders a place to exchange goods, rest, and buy supplies for their journey. Traveling the Silk Road was difficult and dangerous, and eventually a sea route from Europe to China replaced it.

   B Along with paper, spices, and jade, silk was one of the goods that traders sought. They risked their lives crossing hot deserts and climbing tall mountains to obtain silk, and they also had to fight off bandits. Cities such as Bukhara and Samarkand provided resting places for the traders.

   C Traders were willing to travel great distances for silk, taking with them western goods, such as grapes, pomegranates, and colored glass, that were not available in China. Once Europeans learned the secrets of making silk, they stopped traveling to China as frequently.

   D The Silk Road was a route between China and Europe, joining the city of Xi'an in eastern China with the Mediterranean Sea. It was more than 5,000 miles long. The midpoint of the journey was located in Central Asia. The route, which was made of camel paths and horse trails, passed through inhospitable country, including the world's highest mountains and hottest deserts.

10   Which sentence expresses the central idea of the passage?

   A The Silk Road was an important trade route that helped to enrich the people of China.

   B In the 14th century, the life of a trader was difficult and dangerous.

   C Many ideas are explained in the form of legends handed down from generation to generation.

   D Silk cloth was an important trade commodity for thousands of years.

Supporting Details

Review the Standards (RI.8.2, RI.8.3, RH.8.3, RST.8.3)

- Analyze the development of central ideas through **supporting details**
- Analyze how a text uses **comparisons, analogies,** or **categories**
- Identify **key steps in a process**

Q: How do I find **supporting details**?

A: Supporting details are the main pieces of information that help to explain, prove, or develop the work's central idea. To identify supporting details, ask, *What information does each paragraph give to support the work's central idea?* or *What details in this paragraph support the paragraph's central idea?*

Q: Why do texts use **comparisons, analogies,** and **categories**?

A: Texts use **comparisons, analogies,** and **categories** to show how things are alike or different. The following questions will help you understand how ideas in a text are related:

- What people, ideas, or events are being compared?
- Does the author make an idea clearer by showing how two things are alike?
- Does the passage group people, ideas, or events into categories?
- What defines each category?

Q: How do I identify **key steps in a process**?

A: The **key steps in a process** are the main actions that a person takes to complete a process or procedure. A passage may organize the steps using signal words such as *first, second,* and *so on.* Some passages use a numbered list or a flowchart that shows the order of the steps. Here is a flowchart showing the process of a volcanic eruption.

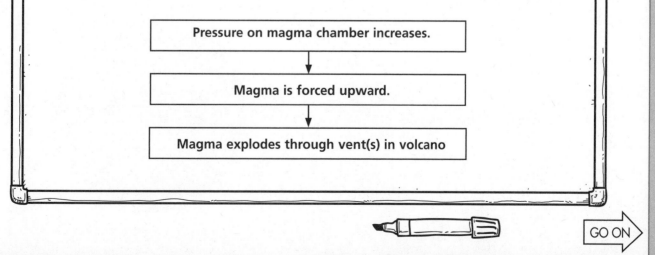

Pressure on magma chamber increases.
↓
Magma is forced upward.
↓
Magma explodes through vent(s) in volcano

GO ON ➡

Directions: Read the passage. Then answer the questions that follow.

Ping-Pong-Zap!

1   Video games are big business. In the year 2009, sales of video games in the United States reached $9.9 billion. The games have become popular for all ages, appealing to all kinds of people from kindergartners to doctors.

The First Video Game

2   Unlikely as it seems, the first video game was not designed for mass sales. In 1958, William Higinbotham was an instrument designer for the Brookhaven National Laboratory. Every fall that lab had an open house. Higinbotham wanted to show the public something with action, so he and Robert Dvorak invented a simple game using an oscilloscope—a device that looks like an air-traffic control screen. The player used a dial and a button to control a solid line to deflect the "ball"—a blip that would bounce when it touched the line. Higinbotham called the game "Tennis for Two." The game was a hit at the open house. Years later, Higinbotham commented, "If I had realized just how significant it was, I would have taken out a patent and the U.S. government would own it!"

The First Home Video Game

3   Although his invention is considered by most people to be the first video game, Higinbotham doesn't receive credit for being the inventor of the *home* video game. That title goes to Ralph Baer, who was an engineer for a military electronics company. In 1966, he designed a more compact tennis game. His blips and lines worked the same way, but he developed a game controller that could be hooked to a television set and that would allow dozens of games to be played. He sold his ideas to Magnavox, who marketed the first home video game system. Soon the Atari Corporation picked up the idea and added several new games. The home video game industry was up and running.

Games Galore

4   Video game technology has come a long way from those early single player, one-dimensional games. Along the way, Nintendo introduced the Game Boy, popularizing handheld gaming. Because of the Internet, players have greater access to online games and have the ability to play against people all over the world in real time through multiplayer online games (MMOs). The newest technology eliminates controllers by utilizing motion sensitive remotes that allow players to move their avatars by moving their own bodies.

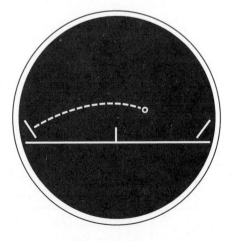

Other Applications

5   Doctors and soldiers are among those using video games for work instead of entertainment. A hospital in Toronto is experimenting with using the Xbox Kinect to virtually manipulate medical images during surgery. The military is finding that it is more cost-effective to alter video game controllers and use them to operate small robotic ground vehicles used for reconnaissance than to build controllers from scratch. There is no doubt that video games will continue to have a big part in American's lives—both at work and at home.

1   The supporting details under the heading **The First Video Game** explain all the following EXCEPT—

   A why the first video game was created.

   B what the game was like.

   C how Higinbotham got rich from designing video games.

   D where the first video game was created.

2   What is the purpose of the section called **Games Galore**?

   A to explain how complex games are developed.

   B to explain how to become a video game tester.

   C to predict the types of video games that will be developed in the future.

   D to describe recent video game technology.

To answer **Example 1**, you must decide which **detail** is NOT contained in the section called **The First Video Game**. A quick reread of this section will show that the only detail which is not included is how Higinbotham got rich from designing video games. **Choice C is correct.**

Example 2 asks about the purpose of the category, or section, called **Games Galore**. It describes the some of the more recent developments in video games. The correct answer is **choice D**.

◎ Try It On Your Own

4   Explain how Ralph Baer's video game was different from Higinbotham's game. (3 points)

_____

_____

_____

_____

_____

GO ON →

5 The flowchart below lists steps in the history of video games.

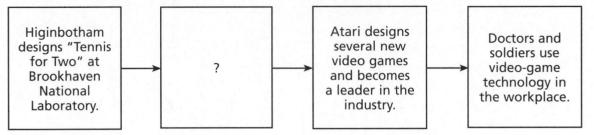

Higinbotham designs "Tennis for Two" at Brookhaven National Laboratory. → ? → Atari designs several new video games and becomes a leader in the industry. → Doctors and soldiers use video-game technology in the workplace.

Which of the following statements belongs in the missing box?

A Nintendo introduces the Game Boy.

B Ralph Baer designs a tennis game that uses a TV controller.

C Sales of video games exceeded $9 billion in 2010.

D The Internet allows people to play against people all over the world.

6 Read the following statement.

The United State Army actually set up a video-game studio to produce games used in training soldiers.

Under which heading would this statement best fit?

A The First Video Game

B The First Home Video Game

C Games Galore

D Other Applications

Test-Taking Tips

1 Go back to the passage to find evidence, such as supporting details, to support an inference or analysis of the text.

2 To make an inference, think about what the text says. Ask, *Which answer follows most logically from details in the text?* or *Based on what the text says, what conclusion can I draw?*

3 To answer questions about the central idea, carefully read the title and introductory paragraph of the text. One or both of these places usually state or give clues to the central idea.

4 When creating a summary, include only the most important ideas or events. Leave out minor details. Keep it concise!

5 To analyze how people, ideas, or events are alike, look for comparisons, analogies, and categories. Ask, *What do these people, ideas, or events have in common?* or *What details help to explain why these people, ideas, or events are grouped in the same category?*

6 Watch for words that signal the order of steps in a process or procedure, such as *first, second, before, after,* and *last.* Check to see if the text gives a list or flowchart showing the order of the steps.

Go for it!

Unit Three Practice Test   Estimated time: 25 minutes

Directions: Read each passage and answer the questions that follow.

Artificial Intelligence

1 Watch any science fiction movie and you'll see computers that think and act on their own. However, computers with artificial intelligence, or AI, are no longer a thing of science fiction. AI is currently at the forefront of computer technology. As AI scientists probe into the future, they ask themselves questions that will define their science for the coming years. How can we move beyond the instructional programming of computers and create machines that can think? How can we create machines that can reason, interpret, analyze, make judgments, and more?

2 To answer these questions, AI scientists must consider the ways in which people learn. One way we learn is by solving problems. We generally do this with a two-step process. First, we check the facts; second, we use our reasoning abilities to come up with solutions. Scientists have simulated this problem-solving capability by creating *expert systems*. These highly sophisticated systems are composed of a *knowledge base* (facts) and an *inference engine* (reasoning ability).

3 In 2011, Watson, an IBM supercomputer, beat two champions at the game of *Jeopardy*. Watson has a 3,000-computer processor brain that can perform several tasks simultaneously. Watson has the ability to understand a question, analyze it, and then search the Internet for the answer. To some extent, Watson also has the ability to learn. Suppose Watson searches for information on the U.S. president shot in 1901. It sends off many algorithms searching for the answer. When one of the algorithms returns with the statement "William McKinley was a U.S. president shot in 1901," Watson's confidence index for that algorithm increases. In this way Watson learns which algorithms will be more successful in finding answers to certain types of questions.

4 It has taken scientists over 50 years to develop a computer with Watson's level of artificial intelligence. In 1951, a British computer scientist developed one of the first game-learning programs for checkers. In 1954, two MIT researchers created successful simulations of brain neurons—enabling computers to "think" and "learn" by recognizing patterns. Next, scientists developed a computer that could recognize and understand language. In the late 1960s, Skakey the Robot was the first computer to use vision and touch sensors to explore an environment, make a plan to achieve a goal, monitor the execution of the plan, and make corrections as needed. Finally in 1997, IBM's Deep Blue chess computer defeated chess grandmaster Gary Kasparov.

5 Today, some researchers define artificial intelligence as systems that "efficiently perform tasks assigned by humans." According to this definition, artificial intelligence is all around us—in motion-sensing gaming systems, in vaccums that can be programmed to clean on their own, and in cell phones that respond to voice commands. However, researchers still dream of building a machine that can do all the cognitive things that humans can. This original definition of artificial intelligence continues to be the goal of many scientists.

1 The main idea of the passage is—

   A Artificial intelligence is now a reality.

   B People learn by solving problems, but computers can't yet solve problems.

   C Watson is a supercomputer that can think on its own.

   D Artificial intelligence is the science of creating computers that can think like humans can.

2 The purpose of Paragraph 4 is to—

   A explain why Watson was created.

   B detail scientific developments in technology of artificial intelligence.

   C give the history of the personal computer.

   D explain reasons why scientists want to develop artificial intelligence.

3 Write a summary of "Artificial Intelligence." Include the central idea and key supporting details. (3 points)

_____

_____

_____

_____

_____

_____

_____

_____

_____

_____

_____

_____

_____

_____

_____

_____

_____

4 Which statement describes an inference you can make after reading the passage?

   A Scientists must program computers to be able to think and make decisions.
   B Scientists are close to developing computers that can experience human emotions.
   C The science of artificial intelligence does not have practical implications for the average person.
   D Computers will never be able to think on their own.

5 In the process of solving problems, what is the second step mentioned in the article?

   A create expert systems
   B use reasoning abilities to come up with solutions
   C consider the ways in which people learn
   D check the facts

6 Paragraph 5 states that some researchers define artificial intelligence as systems that "efficiently perform tasks assigned by humans." How is this definition different from the definition of artificial intelligence given in Paragraph 1? Which definition do you feel Watson is an example of? Support your answer with examples from the text. (3 points)

_____

_____

_____

_____

_____

_____

_____

_____

_____

_____

_____

_____

_____

_____

STOP

Points Earned/Total = _____ /10

Reading Informational Text Lesson 8

Structure and Point of View

Review the Standards (RI.8.5, RI.8.6, RH.8.5, RH.8.6, RST.8.5, RST.8.6)

- **Analyze** and explain how sections, paragraphs, or sentences of a text develop key ideas
- Identify and explain **text structures** such as compare and contrast, cause and effect, or sequence of events
- Determine an author's **point of view** or **purpose** for writing part of or an entire text

Q: How do parts of a text help develop key ideas?

A: To analyze how a part of a work helps develop a key idea, ask, *Why did the author include this part? How does this part help me understand the text as a whole? Does it build on the idea before it? Does it introduce or explain a key supporting idea? Does it give a supporting detail or example?*

Q: How do I explain **text structures**?

A: To answer questions about **text structures**, think about how the ideas in the text relate to one another. The chart below explains common text structures.

Organizational Structure	Description
Compare and Contrast	Ideas are presented so readers see the ways they are alike and the ways they are different. Key words: *however, in contrast, on the other hand*
Sequence of Events or Chronological Order	Ideas are related by time order. Key words: *first, next, later, finally*
Cause and Effect	Ideas are presented so readers can see why something happens and what the consequences are. Key words: *because, so, since, as a result*

Q: How can I determine the author's **point of view** or **purpose**?

A: *Purpose* is related to why the author is writing a text. Common purposes include writing to describe, to persuade, or to give information. The author's **point of view** is his or her opinion on the subject.

Directions: Read the passage. Then answer the questions that follow.

The Video Game: Friend or Foe?

Parents and teachers often express concerns about the amount of time teenagers spend playing video games, and they may have good reason. A study published in 2007 shows that the average adolescent male plays eight hours of video games a week, in sessions that average an hour. But what effect does this have? Are video games actually harming today's teens?

The Benefits

Contrary to popular belief, video games do produce some good results. As early as 1995, social scientists pointed out that the games help teens adapt to a technologically changing world. Frequent players adjust more quickly to new technology and develop improved eye-hand-ear coordination. Also, some games provide learning opportunities as well as entertainment. In 2011, researchers found that the more kids played video games, the more creative they were in tasks such as drawing pictures and writing stories.

The Drawbacks

Despite these benefits, critics are quick to point out the negative effects of video games. Excess body weight has been linked to frequent play, as has poor performance at school. Some students become compulsive players, allowing video games to consume time they might devote to other pursuits, such as sports or homework. Even more disturbing, a 2010 case study found that violence on the screen can cause young adults to become more aggressive in the real world.

Thus, video games appear to be a mixed blessing, offering entertainment and technical prowess while at the same time posing numerous risks. As with any mixed blessing, moderation may be the key. Teens who combine moderate video game use with other activities have a good chance of reaping the benefits while avoiding the detriment of video games.

---

1   Study the chart below.

Cause ⟶	Effect
	poor school performance

Choose the information that <u>best</u> completes the empty portion of the chart.

A staying up late at night

B frequent play of video games

C spending too much time playing sports

D the world changing because of technology

GO ON ⟶

2 The author included the section **The Drawbacks** to support the idea that—

    A negative effects of video games do not outweigh the positive effects.

    B no one knows if video games are friends or foes.

    C video games may have negative effects on users.

    D video games help users to adapt to new technology.

3 The author wrote this passage mainly to—

    A persuade readers to play video games.

    B inform readers about new technology.

    C tell an exciting story about a video game.

    D explain some pros and cons of video games.

4 What is the author's point of view on video games? Use details from the passage to support your answer. (3 points)

_____

_____

_____

_____

_____

Some questions ask you to think about text **structure**, or organization. **Example 1** asks you to identify one of the causes of poor school performance by those who play video games. The passage says that "excess body weight has been linked to frequent play, as has poor performance at school." So **Choice B**, frequent play of video games, is correct.

Authors sometimes arrange a passage in **sections**. To answer **Example 2**, you can use the header **The Drawbacks** as a clue that the section explains something negative or undesirable about video games. Based on the section's description of negative effects on users, you know that **Choice C** is the best answer. The ideas in Choices A, B, and D are not discussed in **The Drawbacks**.

Example 3 asks about the **author's purpose**, or why the author wrote the passage. The passage gives information about video games and arranges the information in two main sections: **The Benefits** and **The Drawbacks**. These sections explain the pros and cons of video games, so **Choice D** is correct.

For **Example 4** you determine the author's **point of view**, or what the author thinks about the topic he or she is writing about. A good response includes at least two details from the passage to support your answer.

Good: *In the first paragraph, the author asks a question: "Are video games actually harming today's teens?" The author's point of view on video games is neither all good nor all bad. It is balanced. You can tell this because he gives both the good points and the bad points of playing video games, or as he calls them, The Benefits and The Drawbacks. This creates a balanced, objective approach and viewpoints. In the conclusion, the author summarizes that video games are a "mixed blessing."*

This is a poor response because it doesn't use details or examples from the passage to support the answer.

Poor: *The author doesn't have a strong point of view one way or another. This isn't really a persuasive passage. It's not trying to get readers to believe something or do something. It is just giving information about the topic.*

◎ Try It On Your Own

5   What does the passage propose as a solution to the dangers of video games for adolescents? Explain your answer on the lines below. (3 points)

_____

_____

_____

_____

_____

_____

_____

_____

_____

_____

6   According to the passage, the most recent study reported that—

   A kids who played video games were more creative.
   B video games can lead to violence.
   C game players adapt more quickly to changes in technology.
   D game players develop improved hand-eye coordination.

7   The author's purpose in writing the section titled **The Benefits** is to—

   A explain that there are no benefits to playing video games.
   B persuade readers that the benefits outweigh the drawbacks.
   C ask the question "Are there benefits to playing video games?"
   D explain some of the benefits of playing video games.

8   The author uses the first sentence in the passage to—

   A express a point of view on the topic.
   B contrast the positive and negative effects of video games.
   C introduce the topic of the passage.
   D convince readers to play video games.

GO ON ▷

Reading Informational Text Lesson 9

Visual Formats

Review the Standards (RI.8.7, RH.8.7, RST.8.7)

- Evaluate **charts** and **graphs** used to communicate information
- **Integrate** and compare and contrast information from **visual formats** with other information in print

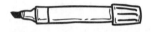

Q: How do I evaluate **charts** and **graphs**?

A: Charts and **graphs** are ways to visually organize information so that readers can understand it quickly. To evaluate these visual formats, decide what idea or facts they show. Read titles or labels that tell you what the numbers, images, or words explain or represent.

Q: How do I figure out what the **visual** information has to do with the information in print?

A: To answer questions about **visual** and printed information, think about how the two sources of information are alike and different. Also consider how the visual information helps you to understand the written information. Does it supply additional facts or figures? Does it show you the size or layout of an object or place described in the text? Asking these questions will help you integrate information from both visual and print sources.

⮕ Try It

Directions: Read the passage. Then answer the questions that follow.

Daylight Saving Time

For most of the United States, Daylight Saving Time (DST) begins at 2 A.M. on the second Sunday of March. At this time, Americans turn their clocks ahead one hour. They trade one hour of daylight in the morning for an extra hour of daylight in the evening. They turn their clocks back one hour on the first Sunday of November, when light during the dark winter months is more precious in the morning than in the evening.

The extra hour of light in the evenings during DST saves energy. When it is light outside, people are less likely to turn on the lights in their homes. They also spend more time outdoors. This means their TV sets and stereos are turned off.

United States and European Daylight Saving Schedules

| | United States | | European Union | |
Year	DST Begins 2 A.M.	DST Ends 2 A.M.	ST† Begins 1 A.M. GMT*	ST Ends 1 A.M. GMT*
2012	Mar. 11	Nov. 4	Mar. 25	Oct. 28
2013	Mar. 10	Nov. 3	Mar. 31	Oct. 27
2014	Mar. 9	Nov. 2	Mar. 30	Oct. 26
2015	Mar. 8	Nov. 1	Mar. 29	Oct. 25
2016	Mar. 13	Nov. 6	Mar. 27	Oct. 30

†Summer Time
* Greenwich Mean Time

Benjamin Franklin was the first to conceive the idea for DST. Franklin was a diplomat in France at the time. He explained his idea in an essay titled "An Economical Project," which was published in 1784. While some people liked Franklin's ideas, others thought that changing the time was a foolish thing to do, especially farmers who rose before dawn and wanted the extra hour for work in the morning.

The idea for DST resurfaced again when William Willet, a London builder, noticed that the beautiful summer sunlight seemed to be wasted in the morning because most people were sleeping. In 1907, Willet wrote a pamphlet about his observations called "Waste of Daylight." Willet suggested advancing the clocks 20 minutes on each of four Sundays in April and turning them back by the same amount on four Sundays in September. Willet passed away in 1915, but the following year a bill called "Summer Time" was drafted and introduced to the British Parliament. The bill was rejected because British farmers were outraged at the idea of Summer Time. But the idea had gained momentum, and by 1916, clocks in Britain were set ahead one hour during the summer.

Summer Time helped the British conserve energy—so much so that they eventually decided to turn their clocks ahead two hours in the summer and one hour in the winter. This was referred to as Double Summer Time.

In 1918, the U.S. Congress passed a law establishing DST to help conserve energy and resources during World War I. DST began on the last Sunday of April and ended on the last Sunday in October. However, DST became unpopular, and by 1919 the law was repealed.

GO ON

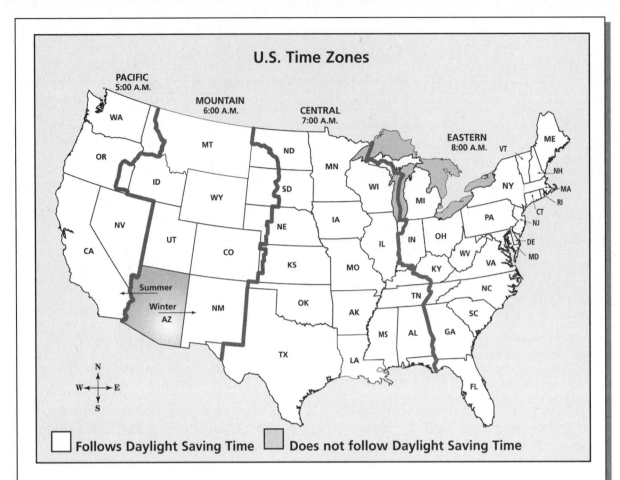

U.S. Time Zones

Follows Daylight Saving Time ☐   **Does not follow Daylight Saving Time** ☐

It wasn't until the United States entered World War II in 1942 that the country again enacted DST. This law remained in effect until 1945, when Congress allowed individual states to choose whether to enact DST. Some states moved their clocks ahead and others didn't. This caused great confusion in the transportation and broadcasting industries.

In 1966, Congress stepped in. It established the Uniform Time Act and set a standard for DST in each time zone in the United States. It exempted only Hawaii, Indiana, and Arizona from having to use DST. Indiana has only recently begun following DST.

To conserve even more energy, in 1986 President Ronald Reagan passed a law that changed DST from the last Sunday in April to the first Sunday in April. It is estimated that the additional month saved the United States about 300,000 barrels of oil a year.

In 2005, President George W. Bush signed the Energy Policy Act that again changed the dates of DST. Beginning in 2007, DST changed from the first Sunday of April to the second Sunday in March. The act also switched the end of DST from the last Sunday in October to the first Sunday in November. Congress passed this law to save the United States even more in energy costs.

1 What feature of the selection shows how many states are in the Central Time Zone?

    A map

    B chart

    C introduction

    D conclusion

2 What is the function of the chart that accompanies this selection?

    A It tells which parts of the United States and the European Union observe Daylight Saving Time.

    B It compares the starting and ending dates of Daylight Saving Time in the United States and the European Union.

    C It explains when Daylight Saving Time ends in the European Union.

    D It defines the phrase "Greenwich Mean Time" for readers.

3 Compare and contrast the information in the chart United States and European Daylight Saving Schedules to the information given in the text. Explain how the visual format gives information that the text does not give. (3 points)

_____

_____

_____

_____

_____

_____

_____

_____

To answer **Example 1**, you must understand **visual formats**, such as charts and graphs, that are used in nonfiction selections to enhance the communication of information. Choices C and D are features of many informational selections but are not graphic features. If you examine the map and the chart included with the selection, you can quickly see that the map shows the states of the United States. When you examine the map, you see that the Central Time Zone is clearly marked. **Choice A is correct.**

Example 2 asks about another type of visual format, a **chart**. A chart is a way to organize information so it can be understood quickly. The title of the chart tells you that it is a schedule. The chart includes two main headings: **United States** and **European Union**. Under these headings is information about when Daylight Saving Time starts and ends each year in the United States and when Summer Time starts and ends in the EU. **Choice B is correct.**

Example 3 asks you to compare and contrast information in a visual source and the print source of information. A good response includes an example from each source of information—visual and print—to support your answer.

Good: *The table lists the beginning and end dates of Daylight Saving Time in the United States and the European Union for the years 2012–2016. The text explains that DST begins in March and ends in November for the United States, but it doesn't give the specific dates. By looking at the chart, you can see that the start dates in the United States range from March 8–13, depending on the year. Likewise, the end dates range from November 1–6.*

This is a poor response because it doesn't use details or examples from the passage to support the answer.

Poor: *The chart is a visual source of information, and the passage uses words to explain some, but not all, of the same information. As you can see, the chart gives more details than the text gives.*

◎ Try It On Your Own

4 According to the chart, what do Daylight Saving Time and Summer Time have in common?

   A Both begin on the same date every year.

   B Both end on the same day each year.

   C Both last for approximately the same amount of time.

   D Both begin at the same hour of day.

5 The map of U.S. time zones develops ideas in the text by showing—

   A when the states in each time zone begin and end Daylight Saving Time.

   B how the time in each zone differs from the time in other zones, whether or not it is DST.

   C how Daylight Saving Time in the United States differs from Summer Time in Europe.

   D what states experienced confusion in the transportation and broadcasting industries.

6 Compare and contrast the information in "U.S. Time Zones" to the information given in the text. Explain how the visual format gives information that the text does not give. (3 points)

_____

_____

_____

_____

_____

_____

_____

_____

_____

_____

_____

_____

_____

_____

_____

_____

_____

Test-Taking Tips

1 To answer questions about how parts of a text develop key ideas, ask, _How does this section support the main idea of the passage? Does it give background information or history? Does it define key terms?_

2 Questions about text structures may ask you to identify or explain a comparison, a cause and effect, or a sequence of events. Look for words that signal text structures such as _because, next, since,_ and _on the other hand._

3 To figure out an author's point of view, think about his or her opinion on the subject. Look for words with positive connotations, such as _great_ and _best,_ or negative ones, such as _poor_ and _worst._

4 To answer questions about visual formats, read any titles, headings, and labels. Look for connections between the chart or graph and the text. Ask, _Does this visual format explain information stated in the text? Does it give additional data? How would my understanding of the passage be different if this visual format were not included?_

Go for it!

Unit Four Practice Test

Estimated time: 20 minutes

Directions: Read the following passage. Then answer the questions that follow.

How to (Scientifically) Make Music

Music is organized sound. So without sound, there is no music. Whether the instrument is a finely crafted violin or merely a bucket turned upside down to create a drum, every musical instrument depends on vibrations to produce sound.

Vibrating Air

To visualize a vibration, think about what happens when you drop a stone into still water. The stone falls and ripples appear, moving away from the spot of contact. The same thing happens when you make music. Say you hit a drum. Air ripples away from the point of contact. These ripples keep moving through the air until they hit something, like a listener's ear. Scientists call the ripples *sound waves*.

Pitch and Frequency

Of course, the point of music is that you can make a variety of sounds—not just one. Musicians refer to the pitch of a sound, or how high or low the note sounds. Scientists refer to a sound's frequency, which is the number of times a sound wave goes through a complete cycle in one second. A cycle is a wave's journey going from its highest point, through its lowest point, and back to its highest point again, like a wave in an ocean. If a sound has a high frequency, meaning its waves are moving quickly, it has a high pitch. If it has a low frequency, or slow-moving waves, it has a low pitch.

Volume

The volume of sounds is also important to music. This is dependent on vibrations as well. A loud sound is said to have a high amplitude, which means the height of its sound waves is larger than a soft sound. Waves that are short have a low amplitude and could be so soft you'd have to strain to hear them.

Timbre

One last feature of vibrations creates the difference between the sound produced by a clarinet and the sound produced by a trumpet. Every musical instrument has its own timbre, or tone color. Timbre is created by the shape of a sound wave. Only tuning forks have perfectly smooth sound waves. Every other instrument—including the human voice—has its own unique shape with jags and bends in each cycle. You can see two examples of these unique shapes in the illustration.

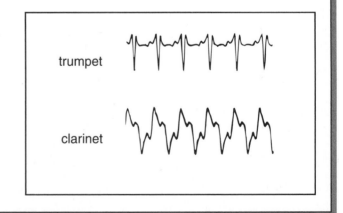

A. high frequency, high amplitude	B. high frequency, low amplitude
C. low frequency, high amplitude	D. low frequency, low amplitude

1 How is the information in this selection organized?

   A in chronological order

   B by problem and solutions

   C by topic and subtopic

   D from most important to least important

2 The purpose of this text is to—

   A persuade the reader to play a musical intrument.

   B inform the reader about how musical sound is made.

   C tell the story of a famous musician.

   D describe what different musical instruments sound like.

3 The section **Vibrating Air** is developed by—

   A making a comparison between sound waves and ripples in water.

   B defining the term *vibration*.

   C showing a picture of sound waves produced by a trumpet and by a clarinet.

   D explaining the relationship between volume and amplitude.

4 The chart illustrating four types of sound waves explains information found in which section(s) of the passage?

   A Vibrating Air

   B Pitch and Frequency

   C Vibrating Air and Timbre

   D Pitch and Frequency and Volume

GO ON

5 Which information from the text supports the idea that illustration B may show a sound that is hard to hear?

   A Frequency is the number of times a sound wave goes through a complete cycle in one second.

   B Sound waves that are short can be extremely soft.

   C Timbre, or tone color, is created by the shape of the sound wave.

   D A slow-moving sound wave has a low pitch.

6 Using evidence from the text, describe the sound explained by illustration A. Then give an example of a sound that would fit this illustration. (5 points)

_____

_____

_____

_____

_____

_____

_____

_____

_____

_____

_____

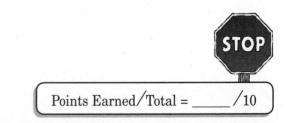

Points Earned/Total = _____/10

Reading Informational Text Lesson 10

Reasons and Evidence

Review the Standards (RI.8.8, RI.8.6, RH.8.6, RH.8.8, RST.8.8)

- Explain an **argument**, specific **claims**, **opinion**, and **facts** in a text
- Evaluate whether the reasoning and evidence is **relevant** and **sufficient**
- Identify irrelevant evidence or avoidance of facts
- Analyze how the author responds to **conflicting evidence** or viewpoints
- Identify how **loaded language** communicates a writer's point of view

Q: How do writers use **arguments** and **claims**?

A: Authors write **argumentative** texts to support **claims** they make. Within the argument, writers also use **facts** and **opinions** to support their claims. For example, a writer may argue that all school lunches should be vegetarian. In support, the writer may claim that eating beef-based entrées leads to weight gain in students. He may support this claim with an opinion from a doctor who promotes an all-vegetable diet and a study that shows vegetarians have lower obesity rates (facts).

Q: How do I know if the reasoning and evidence is **relevant** and **sufficient**?

A: A strong argument relies on facts to support the author's position. To decide whether evidence is **relevant**, ask, *Does this fact or detail clearly and directly relate to the argument or claim?* To decide whether evidence is **sufficient**, ask, *Does the evidence leave unanswered questions? Does it leave room for doubt in the reader's mind?*

Q: How do authors respond to **conflicting evidence**?

A: For every argument, there is an argument for the opposite point of view. Writers sometimes present opposing viewpoints in the text. One reason to do this is to present a balanced picture of the issue. Another reason is to present an opposing viewpoint and then show why it is wrong or weak.

Q: What is **loaded language**?

A: Some words or phrases are "loaded" with emotion. When writers use language such as *evil*, *dangerous*, and *irresponsible*, they are trying to persuade you emotionally. Remember that emotional appeals, such as loaded language, are generally not as persuasive as facts and logical reasons.

GO ON

Directions: Read the passage. Then answer the questions that follow.

Mars Exploration
by Jeremy Nelson

In April 2001, the United States launched the Mars Odyssey space probe to take photos and gather data from Mars. In 2003, 2004, and 2011, NASA sent robotic rovers to Mars. Researchers hope to gather the information needed to attempt a manned mission to Mars within the next few decades. Such a mission will cost billions of dollars. Some people feel that Mars missions are too costly and that exploring Mars will not produce significant benefits for us. These people fail to understand the tremendous significance of the Mars missions. Mars exploration can provide us with critically important information about the formation of the Solar System and the origins of life on Earth.

In order to understand how the Solar System formed, how it evolved, and how it works today, we need to look back in time. The way we can do this most efficiently is by studying the geological formations and chemical compositions of planets' surfaces. By visiting Mars and studying its landscape and soil, we can infer some of the processes of the Solar System's development. If we use Mars as a kind of natural science laboratory, we can learn more about the fundamental physical laws that apply to matter throughout the universe.

Scientists believe that Mars may once have had an atmosphere somewhat like Earth's, and that rivers, lakes, and even small seas may have existed on the planet. Since water plays a vital role in a planet's climate, it is essential that we trace the history of water on Mars and monitor atmospheric conditions there. Doing so may help us predict future climatic changes on Earth.

Another compelling reason to study Mars is to determine if life exists beyond Earth. In 1996, scientists revealed evidence suggesting that some form of bacterial life may have existed on Mars 3.6 billion years ago. While examining a meteorite fragment they believe came from Mars, scientists discovered microscopic forms resembling bacteria fossils. This fragment of rock gives us a tantalizing glimpse of what we might discover on future Mars missions.

We must, therefore, go forward with our exploration of Mars. It is the most important and potentially enlightening scientific quest of our time. What we learn will inform our understanding of the Earth's past, present, and future, and it will make clear our destiny in the grand scheme of the universe.

---

1   Which statement **best** describes the author's central claim?

   A Exploring Mars is essential in order to understand Earth's past, present, and future.

   B Exploring Mars is impossible because it will cost billions of dollars.

   C The Odyssey space probe is the most important space mission ever planned.

   D It is important to explore Mars so people can one day live on that planet.

2 Which statement from the selection is a fact that supports the author's argument in favor of the exploration of Mars?

A *. . . the United States launched the Mars Odyssey space probe to take photos and gather data from Mars.*

B *Such a mission will cost billions of dollars.*

C *In 1996, scientists revealed evidence suggesting that some form of bacterial life may have existed on Mars . . .*

D *It is the most important and potentially enlightening scientific quest of our time.*

3 Which statement expresses an opposing viewpoint offered by the writer?

A Water plays a vital role in the climate of a planet.

B Scientists want to know if there was ever life on Mars.

C Studying other planets may help scientists better understand Earth.

D Exploring Mars may not produce results that are worth the cost.

4 Read this statement from the selection.

These people fail to understand the tremendous significance of the Mars missions.

The writer uses the word *fail* to—

A associate the opposing viewpoint with negative connotations.

B point out an area of the Mars missions needing improvement.

C draw attention to irrelevant information.

D explain why the Mars missions are not a good idea.

5 The writer claims, "Another compelling reason to study Mars is to determine if life exists beyond Earth." Explain whether the author gives relevant evidence to support this claim. (3 points)

_____

_____

_____

_____

_____

   Example 1 asks you to identify the writer's **central claim**. In this selection, the author is clearly arguing in favor of the exploration of Mars, so you can easily eliminate Choice B, which states a reason *not* to explore the planet. The other three choices are all statements in favor of exploring Mars. However, there is no evidence in the text that the author thinks either Choice C or D is true. The only statement that sums up the author's position on the issue is choice A, *Exploring Mars is essential in order to understand Earth's past, present, and future.* **Choice A** is correct.

To answer **Example 2**, you must identify **factual evidence** that supports the author's argument. The correct answer must first be a fact rather than an opinion. When you look at the answer choices, you can see that all choices except Choice D are facts. So the next step is deciding which fact supports an argument in favor of exploring Mars. The only choice that makes sense is C. The fact that scientists found evidence that bacteria may have lived on Mars helps to support the argument that exploring Mars is important in order to learn more about Earth. **Choice C** is correct.

In **Example 3**, you are asked to identify a **conflicting viewpoint** offered by the writer. You already know he is arguing in favor of exploring Mars. Your task is to identify the statement that could be used as evidence in support of *not* exploring Mars. The only statement that does this is Choice D, *Exploring Mars may not produce results that are worth the cost*. The author offers this counterargument when he states that "such a mission will cost billions of dollars. Some people feel that Mars missions are too costly and that exploring Mars will not produce significant benefits . . . " However, he then goes on to say that people who believe this don't understand the full significance of Mars exploration. **Choice D** is correct.

Example 4 asks you to think about how **loaded language** communicates the writer's viewpoint. The word *fail* has negative connotations. By associating the word *fail* with those who oppose his viewpoint, the author reinforces the idea that his argument is valid and the opposing viewpoint is incorrect or faulty. **Choice A** is correct.

To write an answer to **Example 5**, you must evaluate whether the evidence provided is relevant to the following claim: "Another compelling reason to study Mars is to determine if life exists beyond Earth." A good response includes at least two examples from the passage to support your answer.

Good: *The writer claims that we should study Mars to find out "if life exists beyond Earth." The writer supports his claim with two facts. First, he states that in 1996, scientists described evidence for bacterial life on Mars 3.6 billion years ago. Second, he states that scientists have found evidence of "microscopic forms resembling bacteria fossils." These are both strong facts that are directly related to the claim that we should study Mars for evidence of life beyond Earth.*

This is a poor response because it doesn't evaluate specific evidence that supports the claim.

Poor: *The writer claims, "Another compelling reason to study Mars is to determine if life exists beyond Earth." If life on Mars did exist, either now or in the past, that would be a great reason to spend billions of dollars to explore the planet. The author does a good job of creating support for his viewpoint.*

◎ Try It On Your Own

---

6 Which statement is an opinion?

  A *In 2003, 2004, and 2011, NASA sent robotic rovers to Mars.*

  B *Such a mission will cost billions of dollars.*

  C *. . . water plays a vital role in a planet's climate . . .*

  D *It is the most important and potentially enlightening scientific quest of our time.*

7 Does the author provide sufficient evidence to support the claim that exploration of Mars is a good idea? Use two details from the passage to support your answer. (3 points)

_____

_____

_____

_____

_____

_____

_____

_____

_____

_____

_____

8 Which detail from the passage is MOST relevant to understanding why scientists think it is important to explore Mars?

A _. . . the United States launched the Mars Odyssey space probe to take photos and gather data from Mars._

B _Such a mission will cost billions of dollars._

C _In 1996, scientists revealed evidence suggesting that some form of bacterial life may have existed on Mars . . ._

D _It is the most important and potentially enlightening scientific quest of our time._

9 Read this sentence from the passage.

It is the most important and potentially enlightening scientific quest of our time.

The author uses the word _enlightening_ to create the feeling that—

A exploring Mars is good and wise.

B science is a noble profession.

C the sun provides light to the universe.

D we live in a time of scientific discovery.

GO ON

Conflicting Texts

Review the Standards (RI.8.9, RH.8.9)

- Analyze texts with **conflicting information**
- Identify where the texts disagree on facts or in **interpretation**
- Analyze the relationship between a **primary** and **secondary source** on the same topic

Q: What is **conflicting information**?

A: Texts by different writers may disagree on facts or in their interpretation of facts or ideas. We say that the information in the text conflicts, or differs. For example, the Wild West hero Calamity Jane states in her autobiography that she rode for the Pony Express in June 1876. Other texts state that she could not have ridden for the Pony Express because that mail service ended in 1861.

Q: What are **primary** and **secondary sources**?

A: A **primary source** is a document or work created by a witness of or participant in events or experiences. Examples are letters, diaries, speeches, and autobiographies. A **secondary source** is a document or work created later, by a person who did not experience the events or experiences. Examples are biographies, textbook chapters, and scholarly articles.

⮌ Try It

Directions: Read each passage. Then answer the questions that follow.

Ragged-Time Music

At the beginning of the 20th century, a new type of music was sweeping across America. People flocked to performances to tap their feet to its lively rhythms and unusual sounds. These new tunes had bouncing bass, irregular melodies, and defined thematic sections. The unique form was called "ragged time" because of its unusual accents and melodies. As piano players and small bands adopted the style, the name was shortened to "ragtime." Soon, people all over America were writing ragtime songs, or "rags." The most famous writer to emerge from this group was an African American named Scott Joplin.

Joplin, a native of Texas, was born sometime between the summer of 1867 and mid-January 1868. From his humble beginnings on the Texas-Arkansas border, he became a shooting star, shining in New York City's musical *Tin Pan Alley* and beyond. During the height of ragtime's popularity, Scott Joplin was considered the "King of Ragtime."

Although ragtime music peaked in popularity in the 1920s, it experienced a revival in the 1970s. A popular 1973 movie about the ragtime era introduced Joplin's music to a large modern audience. The movie's score, which contained Joplin's catchy rag *The Entertainer*, won an Oscar. Suddenly, songs that Joplin had written 70 years earlier were on the popular and classical music charts. Ragtime had secured its place in the culture and history of America, and Scott Joplin was still its king.

The King of Ragtime

1   Scott Joplin was born in 1868 in northeastern Texas. His parents, who had been enslaved before the Civil War, moved the family to Texarkana in 1875. Joplin's interest in music was sparked by his family's music making. By age seven, he was a skilled banjo player. Young Joplin still wished to learn more about music, so his mother arranged for him to have access to the piano in a house where she worked. Joplin's passion and talent soon caught the eye of a local music teacher named Julius Weiss. Weiss gave free instruction to Joplin in piano and music appreciation. Weiss was especially fond of opera, and he passed on to his pupil his passion for this form. As Joplin developed greater skill as a pianist, he began performing for audiences.

2   Around 1890, Scott Joplin moved to St. Louis, where he was exposed to the sound of ragtime music. Energized by this new style, Joplin decided to study further to increase his technical knowledge of music. He enrolled in George R. Smith College to study piano and music theory and to perfect his music notation. He also began tutoring local musicians. Many of his pupils would go on to become famous ragtime composers.

3   Although Joplin enjoyed working as a performer and tutor, he knew that his real gift was composing music. He wrote and published a few pieces in 1896, but it was not until 1899 that he was able to take full credit for his work. It was then that Joplin released *The Maple Leaf Rag*. Joplin wisely secured a one-cent royalty for each sale, something very rare for an African American at that time. *The Maple Leaf Rag* went on to become the most recognizable rag of the era.

www.photos.com

4   Scott Joplin would continue composing popular rags for the rest of his life. However, he gradually began to focus his attention on new, innovative projects. He completed a piece for dancers and a singing narrator called *The Ragtime Dance*. He also experimented with opera

GO ON

and wrote a piece titled *The Guest of Honor*. The work celebrated Booker T. Washington's 1901 dinner at the White House with President Theodore Roosevelt. Joplin assembled a group to perform the opera on an ambitious tour around the United States, but the production was halted when an insider stole the box office receipts. Joplin could not meet the show's payroll and had to cancel the tour. His greatest loss came when all of his possessions, including his sheet music, were confiscated to pay for the traveling group's lodging. Joplin had no other printed copies of his music, and his opera remains lost to this day.

5   In later years Joplin lived in New York City and Chicago. He continued working on rags and other pieces. In 1910, he finally finished his second opera, *Treemonisha*. This opera was about an educated African American woman. Joplin tried several times to stage a full production of the opera, but he was never able to realize his dream. He died in 1917 without ever having seen his piece performed in full.

1 "The King of Ragtime" states that Joplin was born in 1868 in northeastern Texas, but "Ragged-Time Music" states that Joplin—

 A may have been born in 1867.

 B was born in Tin Pan Alley.

 C may have been born in Arkansas.

 D was born during the Civil War.

2 "Ragged-Time Music" highlights Joplin's presence in Tin Pan Alley, but "The King of Ragtime"—

 A reveals that Tin Pan Alley was an insulting nickname.

 B argues that St. Louis was more important than Tin Pan Alley.

 C explains that Tin Pan Alley was never a real place.

 D does not mention Tin Pan Alley.

3 An autobiography is a person's life story written by that person. How would an autobiography of Scott Joplin differ from "The King of Ragtime"?

_____

_____

_____

_____

   Example 1 asks you to identify where the two passages disagree on facts. To answer the question, review what "Ragged-Time Music" states about Joplin's birth. The first sentence in paragraph 2 of the passage lets you know that **Choice A** is correct. The other choices are false statements and do not occur in either passage.

Example 2 is a question about how the two passages interpret the importance of Tin Pan Alley in Joplin's life. By reviewing "The King of Ragtime," you see that the passage does not mention Tin Pan Alley at all. **Choice D** is correct.

To write an answer to **Example 3**, you must think about the difference between an autobiography, which is a type of **primary source**, and a biography, which is a type of secondary source. A good response includes at least two examples from "The King of Ragtime" to support your answer.

Good: *Like "The King of Ragtime," an autobiography would give information about Scott Joplin's life; however, unlike the biography, an autobiography would give information from a personal, first-person viewpoint. For example, "King" gives facts about Joplin's rise to fame, but an autobiography would reveal Joplin's inner thoughts and feelings about his rise to fame. "King" points out experiences that seem important in Joplin's life, but an autobiography would reveal Joplin's own opinions about which events were most important.*

This is a poor response because it doesn't give examples from the passage to support the answer.

Poor: *"The King of Ragtime" is a biography, which means it tells someone's life story. An autobiography also tells someone's life story. The main difference between the two is that a biography is about someone other than the writer, and an autobiography is about the writer himself.*

◎ Try It On Your Own

Directions: Read each passage. Then answer the questions that follow.

from Up from Slavery

Booker T. Washington

So far as I can now recall, the first knowledge that I got of the fact that we were slaves, and that freedom of the slaves was being discussed, was early one morning before day, when I was awakened by my mother kneeling over her children and fervently praying that Lincoln and his armies might be successful, and that one day she and her children might be free. In this connection I have never been able to understand how the slaves throughout the South, completely ignorant as were the masses so far as books or newspapers were concerned, were able to keep themselves so accurately and completely informed about the great National questions that were agitating the country. From the time that

GO ON →

Garrison, Lovejoy, and others began to agitate for freedom, the slaves throughout the South kept in close touch with the progress of the movement. Though I was a mere child during the preparation for the Civil War and during the war itself, I now recall many late-at-night whispered discussions that I heard my mother and the other slaves on the plantation indulge in. These discussions showed that they understood the situation, and that they kept themselves informed of events by what was termed the "grape-vine" telegraph.

Booker T. Washington

Booker T. Washington was born a slave on a plantation in Virginia on April 5, 1856. Despite his humble beginnings, he went on to become one of the African American community's foremost educators, authors, speakers, and political leaders. Perhaps his greatest achievement was his contribution to the formation and development of Tuskegee Normal and Industrial School, a school for blacks.

Washington was just a child during the years leading up to the Civil War and during the war itself (1861–1865). As a child, he was probably unaware of the significance of the events going on around him. Younger than ten years old at the end of the war, the early years in slavery are less important than the fact that he spent his life working on behalf of former slaves, all of whom struggled to integrate into white society.

After an early career as a teacher, Washington became the first president of Tuskegee. Under his leadership, the school grew and thrived, expanding its enrollment, its funding, and its physical property. During Washington's 34 years at the school, it grew from two small buildings to 100 buildings. Enrollment swelled to 1,500 students, with a faculty of nearly 200. At the time of Washington's death on November 14, 1915, the school had an endowment of about $2 million. The school today is known as Tuskegee University and stands as a testament to Washington's leadership and champion of the rights of minorities.

4 Compare and contrast the information about Washington's experience with slavery provided in the autobiography and in the biography. Use at least one detail from each passage to support your answer. (3 points)

_____

_____

_____

_____

_____

5 Which of these statements from "Booker T. Washington" conflicts with information in the excerpt from *Up from Slavery*?

   A *Washington was just a child during the years leading up to the Civil War and during the war itself.*

   B *As a child, he was probably unaware of the significance of the events going on around him.*

   C *Booker T. Washington was born a slave.*

   D *After an early career as a teacher, Washington became the first president of Tuskegee.*

6 Read this statement from "Booker T. Washington."

. . . the early years in slavery are less important than the fact that he spent his life working on behalf of former slaves . . . .

Washington would most likely disagree with this statement because—

   A as a child he did not know that he would one day be a leader.

   B he felt shame about his early years as a slave.

   C his early years made him aware of the horrible conditions of slavery.

   D he did not like to give out details about his early years in slavery.

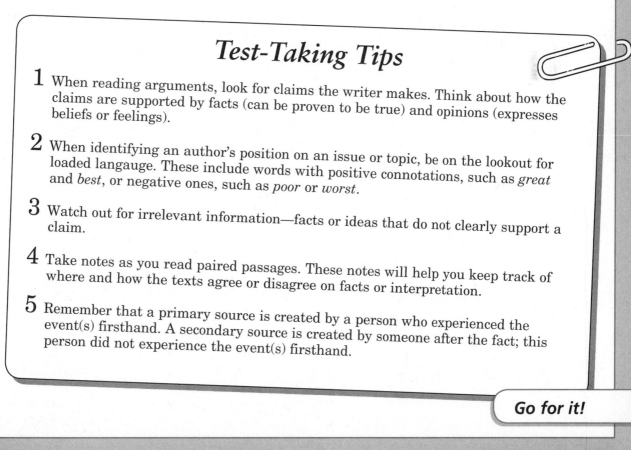

Test-Taking Tips

1 When reading arguments, look for claims the writer makes. Think about how the claims are supported by facts (can be proven to be true) and opinions (expresses beliefs or feelings).

2 When identifying an author's position on an issue or topic, be on the lookout for loaded langauge. These include words with positive connotations, such as *great* and *best*, or negative ones, such as *poor* or *worst*.

3 Watch out for irrelevant information—facts or ideas that do not clearly support a claim.

4 Take notes as you read paired passages. These notes will help you keep track of where and how the texts agree or disagree on facts or interpretation.

5 Remember that a primary source is created by a person who experienced the event(s) firsthand. A secondary source is created by someone after the fact; this person did not experience the event(s) firsthand.

Go for it!

Unit Five Practice Test

Estimated time: 20 minutes

Directions: Read each passage and answer the questions that follow.

The Lyndon B. Johnson Space Center

1 "Houston, we are go for launch."

2 The Florida-based launch team sends this message halfway across the country to Mission Control in Texas. The space shuttle on the launch pad in Florida is ready for liftoff. Final countdown is initiated. Mission Control teams at Houston's Johnson Space Center are ready to direct the shuttle after liftoff.

3 The Johnson Space Center plays a pivotal role in the United States space program today as it has for more than 30 years. It houses the Mission Control Center, provides crew training, and designs and develops new spacecraft.

4 The center traces its beginning to the early 1960s. At that time, the United States was competing with the former Soviet Union to be the first country to send a person into orbit around the Earth. When the Soviets succeeded in 1961, the United States set its sights on sending the first human to the moon. To meet this goal, the United States needed a new center for research, crew training, and flight control. They selected a site about 25 miles from   downtown Houston. Originally named the Manned Spacecraft Center, the new facility opened in September 1963. Ten years later, it was renamed the Lyndon B. Johnson Space Center.

5 Since its opening, the center has served as the nerve center of all human space flights. The center's Mission Control is responsible for communicating with astronauts from the time they launch to the time they land. Technicians monitor systems and crew activities aboard the spacecraft 24 hours a day.

6 The Mission Control Center has two flight control rooms where shuttle missions can be managed. Teams in each flight control room are responsible for different parts of the mission. In each room, huge screens cover the entire front wall. "Call signs" on top of the computer stations identify each person's job. For example, the Flight Director, or "Flight," is the person who leads the flight control team. The spacecraft communicator or "Capcom" is in charge of spacecraft communications. Others analyze data or provide additional support.

7 The work inside Mission Control is only a small part of what goes on at the center. Engineers in another part of the facility design and test all U.S. manned spacecraft, including rockets used in launching shuttles. The space program's earliest rockets were very primitive compared to today's spacecraft. Designs had to change as the program pressed further into space.

8 In 1972 the Center began to develop and test its first space shuttle. Shuttles proved to be much more useful for manned space flight than rockets. Because they have wings like airplanes,

shuttles could land on runways instead of splashing down in the ocean. Their design also helped them serve as science labs. In the future, space shuttles may serve as outposts from which to observe the earth and bases where astronaut can repair satellites. Today, there are four shuttles flying under the direction of the Johnson Space Center.

9   The Johnson Space Center is currently coordinating work on the construction of the International Space Station. The station will act as a permanent orbiting lab, supporting a full-time crew of six. It could also serve as a stopping point on longer journeys to the Moon, Mars, and beyond.

10   The Johnson Space Center has played an important role in our space program almost from the beginning. It will continue to have a prominent role in the coming years, as men and women keep pushing into the unexplored regions of space.

Directions: Use "The Lyndon B. Johnson Space Center" to answer questions 1–3.

---

1   Read this statement from the passage.

The Johnson Space Center plays a pivotal role in the United States space program . . .

Which of these details from the passage is NOT relevant to the claim above?

A *Engineers in another part of the facility design and test all U.S. manned spacecraft . . .*

B *Since its opening, the center has served as the nerve center of all U.S. human space flights.*

C *The center traces its beginning to the early 1960s.*

D *The Johnson Space Center is currently coordinating work on an international space station.*

2   Which statement from the selection expresses an opinion?

A *They selected a site about 25 miles from downtown Houston.*

B *It [the space center] will continue to have a prominent role in the coming years.*

C *Shuttles proved to be much more useful for manned space flight than rockets.*

D *Technicians monitor systems and crew activities aboard the spacecraft 24 hours a day.*

3   Does the author provide sufficient evidence to support the claim that the space center plays a "pivotal role" in the U.S. space program? Why or why not? (3 points)

_____

_____

_____

_____

_____

GO ON

Our Nation's Space Center

The next time you look up into the night sky, notice the Moon. Then, in your mind's eye, travel back down to Earth and find your way to Houston, Texas. What's the connection between these two locations? Houston is home to the primary flight control center that controlled *Apollo 11*, the space flight that landed human astronauts on the moon in 1969. The Lyndon B. Johnson Space Center is our nation's center for human spaceflight training, research, and flight control. Founded in 1963, the center was originally named the Manned Spacecraft Center. It got its new name in 1973, to honor former president Lyndon B. Johnson. The year 2013 marks the space center's 50th anniversary.

A key aspect of the work done at the Johnson Space Center has been finding better ways for humans to work and live in space. As a part of this effort, researchers at the center study other planets. Some scientists, for example, are examining samples collected from space probes.

Another crucial mission of the Johnson Space Center has been to train astronauts. In the earliest days of the space program, seven men were chosen from 500 candidates to train to be space pilots. Today there are about 100 male and female astronauts based at the Johnson Space Center.

www.photos.com

The Johnson Space Center also helped to coordinate work on the International Space Station (ISS). The United States, in partnership with 15 other countries, began building the station in 1998. The ISS is expected to be completed in 2012. Since November of 2000, humans have continuously lived and worked in the space station, which orbits Earth 200 miles above the surface. Each crew provides more information about what it means to live in space for long periods of time.

Some people gripe that the space program is too costly. And unfortunately, the president and Congress seem to agree because in 2011 the government ended the space shuttle project, which was based at the Johnson Space Center for many years. The program was deemed too expensive to continue. Proponents of the idea wish to shift the bulk of human space exploration to private companies. However, these private companies are more interested in profit than scientific discovery. If they do make new discoveries, they are more likely to keep the information private and use it to advance their own causes. America will most likely fall behind other countries in science and technology.

People who think that our money would be better invested in programs such as food relief are shortsighted. One day, perhaps much of our food will be grown on another planet or on a laboratory in outer space.

The work at the Johnson Space Center will continue, but its focus will change. Scientists will develop robonauts to do work in space. The center will also continue to monitor the Mars rovers as they send back data. The scientists there will continue to dream of sending men and women into space.

Directions: Use "Our Nation's Space Center" to answer questions 4–6.

4 The writer responds to the idea that private companies should take over space exploration by suggesting that—

A private companies are more interested in making money than in science.

B private companies won't have the money to send people into space.

C people don't trust private companies.

D NASA won't share its technology with private companies.

5 Read this statement from the passage.

Some people gripe that the space program is too costly.

The writer uses the word *gripe* to suggest that the opposing view is—

A a surprising insight.

B well-reasoned.

C incomplete.

D petty and unimportant.

6 Evaluate the claim that people who think that our money would be better invested in programs such as food relief are shortsighted. Does the writer offer sufficient evidence to support this idea? (3 points)

_____

_____

_____

_____

_____

_____

_____

_____

_____

_____

_____

_____

GO ON

Directions: Use BOTH passages to answer questions 7–9.

7 The two passages give conflicting dates for—

  A when the space center was renamed.

  B when humans first stepped onto the moon.

  C when a human first orbited Earth.

  D the completion of the International Space Station.

8 Which of the following primary sources would most likely provide information on the United States' space program?

  A a speech made by the mayor of Houston, Texas

  B a speech made by Neil Armstrong, the first person to step onto the moon

  C President Lyndon B. Johnson's inaugural speech

  D a speech announcing the Soviets' success in orbiting a person around Earth

9 Identify how the texts offering differing information on the Space Shuttle Program. Why do you think the passages disagree? (3 points)

_____

_____

_____

_____

_____

_____

_____

_____

_____

_____

_____

_____

_____

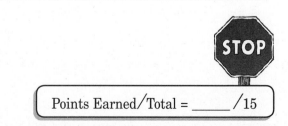

Points Earned/Total = _____ /15

Language Lesson 12

Grammar and Usage

Review the Standards (L.8.1.a–d, L.8.3.a)
- Explain **verbals** (gerunds, participles, infinitives)
- Use **active** and **passive voice** verbs
- Use **indicative**, **interrogative**, **conditional**, and **subjunctive mood**
- Correct **shifts** in **voice** and **mood**

Q: What are **verbals**?

A: Verbals are words that look like verbs but are used as other parts of speech. This chart shows the three types of verbals.

Verbal	Explanation	Example
Gerunds	• end in *-ing* • act as nouns	<u>Drawing</u> is my favorite hobby.
Participles	• most often end in *-ing* or *-ed* • act as adjectives	<u>Running at top speed</u>, I won the race.
Infinitives	• *to* + verb form • act as a noun, adjective, or adverb	I want <u>to eat a hamburger</u>.

Q: What are **active** and **passive voice** verbs?

A: In **active voice**, the subject is doing the action. In **passive voice** verbs, the subject is being acted upon.

Active: Jamal threw the football to Tony.

Passive: The football was thrown by Jamal.

Whenever possible, use active voice to communicate ideas clearly and effectively.

Q: What are **indicative, interrogative, conditional,** and **subjunctive moods**?

A: The **mood** of a verb is the way in which the verb expresses an idea.

Mood	What it does	Examples
Indicative	states a fact	A national park makes a good vacation spot.
Interrogative	asks a question	What makes camping so much fun?

GO ON

Mood	What it does	Examples
Imperative	gives a command or makes a request	Look at this brochure on Yellowstone National Park.
Subjunctive	expresses an idea that is a supposition, a wish, or an idea that is doubtful or uncertain	If I were you, I'd pack a water bottle. I wish I were a better skier. (*I wish I was* and *If I was* are incorrect.)
Conditional	shows that an action is reliant on something else	If we want to make it home before dark, we should leave now.

Q: What are **shifts in mood** and **voice**?

A: When two verbs are in the same sentence, the **voice** of the verb should stay the same.

Incorrect: When the children <u>turned</u> on the TV, a buzzing sound <u>was heard</u>.

Active   Passive

Correct: When the children <u>turned</u> on the TV, they <u>heard</u> a buzzing sound. (both active)

Shifts in mood often happen between indicative and imperative moods.

Incorrect: <u>Try the tamales,</u> and then <u>you should tell me how they taste.</u>

Imperative   Indicative

Correct: <u>Try the tamales,</u> and then <u>tell me how they taste.</u> (both imperative)

⮕ **Try It**

Directions: Choose the best answer for the following questions.

1   Read the following sentence.

I don't want <u>to ride the bus home</u>.

The underlined part is a

A prepositional phrase

B gerund

C infinitive

D participle

2 Which of the following sentences is written in active voice?

   A I hit the ball over the fence.

   B The ball was chased by Lamar.

   C The game was won by the Yankees.

   D The last call was made by the umpire.

3 Which of the following sentences is in the interrogative mood?

   A Hand me the hammer.

   B Did you find the nails?

   C If I were you, I'd wear safety goggles.

   D I wish I hadn't decided to make a bird house.

4 Correct the shift in mood in the following sentence.

Cut off three inches of wood, and then you should sand the end with sandpaper.

_____

_____

_____

For **Example 1**, you must understand **verbals**. The underlined phrase begins with the word *to*. Verbals that begin with *to* are called infinitives. Remember that *to* can also be used to begin a prepositional phrase, such as *to the store*. In an infinitive, *to* is followed by a verb form. The correct answer is **choice C**.

Example 2 tests your knowledge of **active** and **passive voice** verbs. In active voice verbs, the subject is doing the action. In passive voice verbs, the subject is being acted upon. Only in choice A is the subject doing the action. The correct answer is **choice A**.

Example 3 asks you to find the sentence in **interrogative mood**. You need to find the sentence that asks a question. The correct answer is **choice B**.

For **Example 4**, you must identify and correct the **shift** in the sentence. In this case the shift is in the mood of the sentence. The first clause is an imperative. The second clause is indicative. Correct the sentence by changing the second clause to imperative mood.

Good: *Cut off three inches of wood, and then sand the end with sandpaper.*

GO ON

Directions: Choose the best answer for the following questions.

5 Rewrite the following sentence so that it doesn't contain a shift in mood.

We could travel to Arizona where we will see the Grand Canyon.

_____

_____

6 Read the following sentence.

Tired from hiking, the girls crawled into their tents and fell asleep.

The underlined part is a—

A prepositional phrase
B gerund
C infinitive
D participle

7 Rewrite the following sentence so that it is written in active voice.

He was named Rembert Byrd Carter III by his mother.

_____

_____

8 Finish the following conditional sentence.

If we want to buy tickets,—

A we must purchase them today.
B we can purchase them today.
C we will purchase them today.
D purchase them today.

Capitalization, Punctuation, and Spelling

Review the Standards (L.8.2.a–c)

- Use correct capitalization
- Use correct punctuation, including **commas**, **ellipsis**, and **dashes** to indicate a break or pause
- Use correct spelling

Q: How should I use **commas**, **ellipses**, and **dashes** to indicate a pause or break?

A: Ellipses are used in dialogue to indicate the speaker is thinking or that the speaker did not complete his thought.

Example: "Well . . . I don't know who won the election," said the ballot keeper.

Dashes indicate an abrupt change in thought.

Example: I've misplaced my book—oh, I see you have it.

Commas naturally introduce a break or pause in sentence. However, do not use commas whenever you feel like it. Use the following rules as a guide.

Basics of Punctuation

Comma

☞ Use a comma to separate items in a series.

We painted the doors, window frames, and shutters.

☞ Use a comma before the conjunction in a compound sentence.

I picked the color, and my mother bought the paint.

☞ Use a comma to set off introductory words and phrases, appositives, parenthetical phrases, and words of direct address.

Although it looks challenging, I still want to go.
Alexis, have you finished your work?

☞ Use a comma to set off a direct quotation.

Inga said, "I'll go with you."
"Follow me," said the ranger.

Semicolon

☞ Use a semicolon between two independent clauses not joined by a conjunction.

Eat the chicken; the fish is not very good.

Colon

☞ Use a colon before a list.

Three things are on my mind: my homework, my lunch, and my dog.

GO ON ⟶

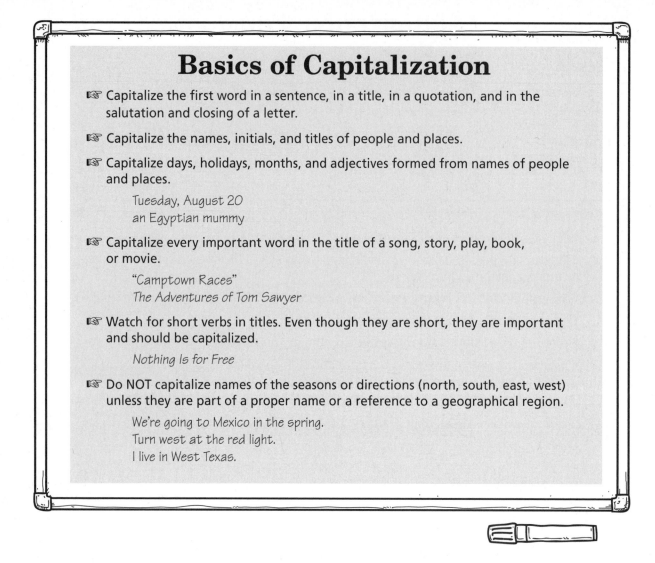

Basics of Capitalization

☞ Capitalize the first word in a sentence, in a title, in a quotation, and in the salutation and closing of a letter.

☞ Capitalize the names, initials, and titles of people and places.

☞ Capitalize days, holidays, months, and adjectives formed from names of people and places.

> Tuesday, August 20
> an Egyptian mummy

☞ Capitalize every important word in the title of a song, story, play, book, or movie.

> "Camptown Races"
> The Adventures of Tom Sawyer

☞ Watch for short verbs in titles. Even though they are short, they are important and should be capitalized.

> Nothing Is for Free

☞ Do NOT capitalize names of the seasons or directions (north, south, east, west) unless they are part of a proper name or a reference to a geographical region.

> We're going to Mexico in the spring.
> Turn west at the red light.
> I live in West Texas.

➲ Try It

Directions: Read each question and choose the best answer.

1 Which of the following sentences does NOT use correct punctuation?

A Please call the police—wait, they're already here.

B "Hmmm . . . I'm not sure how to answer," said Mimi.

C We saw eight—yes, we counted them—deer on the football field.

D I want to eat the entire cake, no, I don't.

2 Which sentence uses correct capitalization?

A *A Wrinkle in Time* is one of Suzanna's favorite Fantasy books.

B It is the first in a series of books written about an american girl named Meg Murray.

C I told Suzanna that she should plan on reading *The Wind in the Door* next.

D The author, Madeleine L'Engle, graduated from Smith college in Massachusetts.

3 Which sentence does NOT include misspelled words?

A James Farmer was an important sivil-rights leader, but he is remembered by few people today.

B He was one of the Freedom Riders who traveled across the South to work for equality.

C In 1999, Farmer was finally rekognized for his contributions to his country.

D He was awarded the Medal of Freedom, the nation's highest civillian honor.

Example 1 tests your knowledge of **dashes**, **ellipses**, and **commas**. Dashes are used to show an abrupt change in thought. They are used correctly in choices A and C. In choice B, ellipses are correctly used to show a pause in a speaker's words. However, in choice D, commas are incorrectly used. A dash should be used instead of the comma after *cake*. The answer is **choice D**.

To answer **Example 2**, you must understand the rules of **capitalization**, including how to capitalize titles, proper nouns, and proper adjectives. Choice A is incorrect because *fantasy* is not a proper adjective, so there is no reason to capitalize it. Choice B is wrong because the word *American* is a proper adjective and must always be capitalized. Choice D is incorrect because the word *college* is part of the name of a specific school, which makes it a proper noun. **Choice C** is correct.

Some test questions will assess your **spelling** ability. When looking for misspelled words, study each sentence to see if any words "look wrong." When you read, you are used to seeing words spelled correctly, so if a word looks wrong, it may be because it is misspelled. In **Example 3**, all sentences but one should have at least one spelling error. In choice A, the word *civil* is misspelled. In choice C, *recognized* is misspelled, and in choice D, *civilian* is misspelled. The only sentence with no misspelled words is **choice B.**

GO ON →

◎ Try It On Your Own

Directions: Read each question and choose the best answer.

4 Which sentence is punctuated correctly?

A When you see an accident, do you know what to do?

B First of all try to call the police.

C Use a cell phone if possible or go to a phone booth.

D The police will get ambulances fire trucks, or any other help needed.

5 Which sentence punctuates dialogue correctly?

A "Stephen," said Andy were there many people in the auditorium?"

B "I'm not sure," Stephen answered, "because I didn't look carefully."

C "I did said Dave and the place looked pretty full to me."

D Well, said Andy, "I guess that means that we can start the show now."

6 Which sentence is punctuated correctly?

A Last year, Arnies father forgot to have the family's mail stopped when they went on vacation.

B Two weeks worth of mail had collected in the mailbox.

C There were many bills' and even more pieces of junk mail.

D "It's a good thing we weren't gone longer," Arnie said.

7 Which sentence is punctuated correctly?

A The camp counselor suggested three dates for the meeting, May 12, June 30, or August 10.

B Franco chose June; I chose August.

C Since we couldn't agree; the counselor made one more suggestion.

D He said: "Shall we just have our meeting right now?"

Go for it!

Unit Six Practice Test

Estimated time: 15 minutes

Directions: Read each question and choose the best answer.

1   Read the following sentence.

Talking with your mouth full is considered rude.

The underlined part of the sentence is a(n)—

A gerund.
B participle.
C infinitive.
D verb.

2   Read the following sentence.

I don't want to catch your cold.

The underlined part of the sentence is a(n)—

A gerund.
B participle.
C infinitive.
D verb.

3   Which of the following sentences has an active voice verb?

A The solo was sung by a professional opera singer.
B Maya played the piano during the concert.
C The play was written by William Shakespeare.
D The dog was walked by my brother.

4   Which of the following sentences is in imperative mood?

A Will you be riding the bus?
B You will be walking to the YMCA after school.
C Stop the bus before it leaves!
D If you miss the bus, then you will walk home.

5   Which sentence does NOT contain an incorrect shift in mood or voice?

A Stephanie Collins writes about futuristic worlds, and readers are captivated by her characters.
B Read the book and then write your report.
C Make your bed, and you should dust your room.
D To earn money, car washes were offered by the band members.

6 Which of the following sentences does NOT use correct punctuation?

A "I don't like to . . . eat sushi," said Jaime.

B The only thing I could do . . .which wasn't much . . . was wait for the ambulance to arrive.

C "I will never, never, never eat sea urchin," cried Jackie.

D Take out the cookies before they burn—oops, too late.

7 Which sentence is punctuated correctly?

A Connie and I went to Mason's Department Store the largest store in the city.

B Women's shoe's are sold on the third floor of the store.

C The first floor is for cosmetics, purses, and belts.

D "I've never been in this store before, said Connie."

8 Which sentence does NOT use correct capitalization?

A I went to a lecture by Professor Tina Torres.

B She quoted from her book *Growing Up in America*.

C She will give another lecture on Wednesday, April 12.

D She is one of the most popular Professors in the school.

9 Which sentence does NOT include misspelled words?

A A remarkable archaeological discovery was made in China.

B Thosands of clay figurines were found buried in the ground.

C Many of the figerines were soldiers of various kinds, some carrying weapons.

D Most of the status were painted in bright colors.

10 Which version of the sentence is punctuated correctly?

A Around the end of the 17th century, people became interested in the idea of a "universal language," one that everyone in the world would speak and understand.

B Around the end of the 17th century: people became interested in the idea of a "universal language," one that everyone in the world would speak and understand.

C Around the end of the 17th century, people became interested in the idea of a "universal language" one that everyone in the world would speak and understand.

D Around the end of the 17th century; people became interested in the idea of a "universal language" one that everyone in the world would speak and understand.

STOP

Points Earned/Total = _____ /10

Language Lesson 14

Context Clues and Reference Materials

Review the Standards (L.8.4.a, L.8.4.c, L.8.4.d, L.8.6)

- Determine the meaning of unknown and multiple-meaning words using **context** clues
- Understand and use academic words and phrases
- Use **reference materials** to check word meaning, pronunciation, and part of speech

Q: How can the **context** of a word help me determine the meaning of a word?

A: The other words and sentences surrounding a word are its **context**. The following chart shows some of the ways a word's context can provide clues to its meaning.

Type of context clue	How it provides a clue	Example
Definition	explains the meaning	An <u>intermittent</u> pain is *one that starts and stops throughout the day.*
Example	illustrates or gives a sample	Our <u>rations</u> for the day included *an apple, a banana, and three sandwiches.*
Restatement	says again with a different word or words	Coyotes can *coexist* with humans. They *live alongside us* in our cities and suburbs.
Contrast	uses an opposite	Unlike my <u>gregarious</u> neighbor, Justin is *quiet and shy.*

Q: How can **reference materials** help me find information about a word?

A: Reference materials include **dictionaries**, **thesauruses**, and **glossaries**.

Dictionaries contain the most complete information about each entry word, including part of speech (noun, verb, adjective), pronunciation, word origins, and all possible meanings.

Glossaries are found in a book and only contain the definitions of words used in the book.

Thesauruses list synonyms, or words with similar definitions, and antonyms, or words with opposite meanings for each entry word.

GO ON

Directions: Read the following passage. Then answer the questions that follow.

The Folklore Project

1   During the Great Depression, millions of American citizens were out of work and destitute. In response, President Franklin D. Roosevelt initiated a group of federal programs to create jobs for the unemployed. These programs collectively came to be known as the New Deal. Many New Deal projects called for manual labor to build roads, dams, or buildings, but a program known as the Folklore Project utilized the skills of many jobless American writers.

2   The Folklore Project sent writers to record the life stories of more than 10,000 Americans from various regions, occupations, and ethnic groups. Writers recorded customs and beliefs regarding marriage, cooking, and religion. One goal of the project was simply to capture the everyday life of ordinary people such as maids, farmers, meat packers, and store clerks. Another goal was to foster tolerance for different groups throughout the country.

3   The interviews were not easy to conduct. Though some of the project's writers had professional writing experience, others had been teachers or office workers. Without the luxury of tape recorders, writers had to take careful notes. They also paid close attention to the way people spoke in order to be able to represent their particular manner of speech.

4   The Folklore Project's life histories were to be published in a series of anthologies. Unfortunately, they were never completed. Soon after the United States entered World War II, all available funds were needed for defense. The project was terminated and the staff disbanded. However, the original manuscripts of the Folklore Project still reside in the Library of Congress, enabling today's researchers, historians, and interested citizens to explore this rich trove of information on life in a bygone era.

www.ArtToday.com

Franklin D. Roosevelt

---

1 Which phrase from the selection helps you understand the meaning of destitute?

   A *American citizens*

   B *out of work*

   C *millions of*

   D *group of federal programs*

2 According to the selection, what is a trove?

   A a religious custom

   B a valuable collection

   C an interested citizen

   D a federal writing project

> **con•duct** (kon-dukt′), [Latin *conductus*] *v.* **1.** to manage or guide
> **2.** to lead musicians in an orchestra **3.** to transmit (electricity)
> (kon′-dukt), *n.* **4.** the way a person acts; behavior

3 Which definition best fits the use of the word <u>conduct</u> in paragraph 3?

  A definition 1

  B definition 2

  C definition 3

  D definition 4

4 Which part of the dictionary entry explains the origin of the word?

  A con•duct

  B (kon-dukt′)

  C [Latin *conductus*]

  D *v.*

Example 1 asks you to identify **context clues**. Context clues are other words in a sentence, or in surrounding sentences, that help you understand a word's meaning. In Example 1, the clue to the meaning of the word *destitute* is the phrase *out of work*. **Choice B** is the correct answer.

Example 2 again asks you to use context clues. However, this time you are asked to think about the meaning of the entire selection. From your reading, you know that the folklore project was intended to gather life histories. You can eliminate choice A. Although the project did collect information about religious customs, that was only one element of the histories. You can also eliminate choice C, since "this <u>trove</u>" clearly refers back to the collection of manuscripts, not to people. Choice D is tricky—the manuscripts *were* part of a federal writing project; however, that is not the meaning of the word *trove*. The best answer is **choice B**, *a valuable collection*.

Examples 3 and 4 test your abilities to use a **dictionary**. A dictionary entry tells you a word's pronunciation, origins, part of speech, and all its definitions.

Example 3 asks you to use context clues to determine the definition of a word. The selection says "the interviews were not easy to <u>conduct</u>." The only definition that makes sense is *definition 1*, "to manage or guide." **Choice A** is correct.

Example 4 asks about the **etymology**, or origin, of the word. English is a language filled with words "borrowed" from other languages. When listing such a word, a dictionary usually indicates what language or languages the word comes from, along with what the actual word is in those languages. The part of the entry in brackets, [Latin *conductus*], gives the origin of *conduct*. So the correct answer is **choice C**.

GO ON

Directions: Use the passage on page 112 to answer the questions that follow.

5   Read the thesaurus entry.

> **TERMINATE**
> *verb*
>
> **circumscribe**   limit in range or scope. *Mom tried to circumscribe our television time.*
>
> **conclude**   finish. *Mr. Malone asked me to conclude the presentation after 30 minutes.*
>
> **demarcate**   limit within certain boundaries. *The marathon course was demarcated using road markers.*
>
> **discontinue**   end before completion. *The car company discontinued production of all cars before it lost more money.*

Which synonym is the best replacement for <u>terminated</u> in paragraph 4?

A circumscribe

B conclude

C demarcate

D discontinue

6   Which phrase from the selection helps you understand the meaning of <u>customs</u>?

A *One goal of the project*

B *maids, farmers, meat packers, and store clerks*

C *beliefs regarding marriage, cooking, and religion*

D *more than 10,000 Americans*

7   As used in the passage the word <u>defense</u> means—

A an argument in support of a position.

B part of a team that prevents an opposing team from scoring.

C a defending party in a court of law.

D part of the government responsible for defending the country.

8   Which of the following sentences uses the word <u>ethnic</u> correctly?

A The U.S. has seen an increase in <u>ethnic</u> minorities emigrating from Eastern Europe and the Middle East.

B His boss praised him for his good work <u>ethnic</u> and then gave him a raise.

C Make sure to <u>ethnic</u> your work before you turn it in.

D The art museum was shocked to find that the statue was not <u>ethnic</u>; it was just an excellent reproduction.

Word Parts and Relationships

Review the Standards (L.8.4.b, L.8.5.b)

- Use Greek and Latin **affixes** and **roots** to determine word meaning
- Use relationships between words to understand both words

Q: How can knowing the meaning of a Greek or Latin **affix** or **root** help me understand a new word?

A: Many English words were originally from Greek and Latin. By understanding the meanings of common word parts (prefixes, **roots**, and suffixes), you can figure out unfamiliar words. For example, knowing that the prefix *mis-* means "not" and the root word *nom* means "name" will help you decipher the meaning of the word *misnomer*, which means "a wrong name or inappropriate term." The following charts contain common Latin and Greek roots, prefixes, and suffixes.

Root	Meaning	Examples
am, amor	love, liking	amiable, enamored
brev	short	brief, abbreviate
dem	people	democracy, epidemic
spir	breath	perspire, respiration

Prefix	Meaning	Examples
auto-	self	automobile, automatic
circum-	around	circumnavigate, circumvent
post-	after	postscript, postdate
re-	again	redo, remake

Suffix	Meaning	Examples
-ar, -er, -or	one who	racer, inspector
-ic	like	heroic, poetic
-ize	make	realize, materialize
-ship	condition	relationship, leadership

GO ON →

Q: How can I determine the relationship between pairs of words?

A: Look at the following word pairs, or word analogies.

WARM : HOT :: cool : cold

The above example reads "Warm is to hot as cool is to cold." In other words, the word *warm* has the same relationship to the word *hot* as the word *cool* has to the word *cold*. To answer analogy questions you should try to figure out the relationship between the first two words. Then read the answer choices and find the answer that most closely fits the relationship of the first two words. In this example, we understand that *hot* is a synonym for *warm*, and *cold* is a synonym for *cool*.

| Common Types of Analogies ||
Analogy	Example
cause : effect	cold : frostbite
word : synonym	mistake : error
word : antonym	strong : weak
part : whole	nose : face
item : category	carrot : vegetable

⊃ **Try It**

Directions: Read the following passage. Then answer the questions that follow.

John Adams, Second President of the United States

1   John Adams was born in Braintree, Massachusetts, just south of Boston. He grew up on the ancestral land that had been first farmed by his great-grandfather. After he began to practice law, he met many leaders in the Massachusetts colony and became involved in government.

2   Along with his cousin Samuel Adams, the well-spoken John Adams was one of the most articulate and vocal opponents of British rule in the American colonies. He firmly believed that the American people must be free of England. In his eyes, there was no hope of reconciliation because the differences couldn't be settled.

3   Adams spent years as a diplomat, serving as representative of the colonies in France and the Netherlands. In 1777, he went on a mission with Benjamin Franklin to gain support for the colonies from France. A few years later he returned to help negotiate, or work out an agreement for, peace at the end of the American Revolutionary War.

4   In 1781, George Washington was chosen as the first president. John Adams was elected vice president. Adams did not have a high regard for the role he held. In fact, he once said the office of vice president was "the most <u>insignificant</u>" ever imagined.

5   Adams later served as second president of the country. He was the first president to live in the White House and the first to have a son who also became president.

John Adams

1   Knowing that the Latin root *voc* means "voice" helps you understand that a "<u>vocal</u> opponent"—

   A is one who speaks out against someone or something.

   B is one who is afraid to speak his or her own mind.

   C has an excellent singing voice.

   D is one who is unable to speak in public.

2   What is the meaning of the prefix *in-* in the word <u>insignificant</u>?

   A extra

   B before

   C more

   D not

3   SUPPORT : ENCOURAGE :: articulate :

   A unknown

   B well-spoken

   C angry

   D evil

In **Example 1**, you must consider the **linguistic root** of the word *vocal*. In this case, you are given the linguistic root for the word vocal—the Latin word *voc*, which means "voice." Knowing this, you understand that a vocal person must be one who uses his or her voice. You can eliminate choices B and D because those mention someone who does NOT use his or her voice. Choice C is also incorrect because using your voice has nothing to do with having a good singing voice. **Choice A**, *one who speaks out against someone or something*, is correct.

Example 2 also tests your understanding of **word origins**. In addition to understanding linguistic roots, it is also helpful to understand the origins and meanings of common prefixes and suffixes derived from other languages. From the context of the passage, you know that Adams didn't think much of being vice president. The correct answer is **choice D**, *not*. Adams thought the office of vice president was not significant.

GO ON

Example 3 asks you to think about the relationship between words used in the passage. The example gives you a **word analogy**. First, think about the relationship between *support* and *encourage*. These are synonyms. You need to find a synonym for the word *articulate*. From the context, you know that John Adams is well-spoken. This is a synonym for *articulate*. The correct answer is **Choice B**.

◎ Try It On Your Own

Directions: Use the passage on pages 116–117 to answer the following questions.

4 PEACE : WAR :: reconciliation :

   A divorce

   B agreement

   C cohabitate

   D happiness

5 Which of the following words does NOT begin with the prefix *op-* meaning "against"?

   A opposite

   B oppose

   C opposition

   D operation

6 FARMER : FARM :: diplomat :

   A negotiate

   B peace treaty

   C rule

   D elect

Test-Taking Tips

1 Context clues may not be in the same sentence as the underlined word. Look at the sentences that come before and after the unknown word too.

2 If you are not sure of the meaning of a prefix or suffix, choose the definition that makes the most sense in the sentence.

3 When choosing among alternate meanings for a word, decide what the underlined word means in the sentence. Then look for the dictionary definition that best matches that meaning. Be sure the alternate word you choose is the same part of speech. For example, "to *conduct*" uses the word as a verb; "bad *conduct*" uses the word as a noun.

Go for it!

Unit Seven Practice Test

Estimated time: 15 minutes

Directions: Read the selection. Then answer the questions that follow.

Flightless Birds

1 When most people think of birds, they picture feathered creatures soaring gracefully through the air. This picture is only partially correct. Though all birds have feathers, not all birds can fly. There are many different types of flightless birds, ranging from the land-loving ostrich to the ocean-dwelling penguin. And within this group of flightless birds, there exists surprising diversity. Sprinting at amazing speeds and fighting off enemies in strange ways, flightless birds are fascinating animals.

2 The ostrich is perhaps the best-known flightless bird. The world's largest bird, it stands nearly eight feet tall with a long, flexible neck. Male ostriches have black feathers and long white plumes; these feathers were once worn by humans as a fashion accessories. Females have dull brown feathers. In order to defend themselves against enemies, ostriches use their sharp eyesight and their lean, powerful legs to see and outrun predators. Ostriches take long steps and can reach speeds of up to 40 mph. If cornered, they can kick and use their two long toes with thick nails to protect themselves. Ostriches feed mainly on plants, but they eat sand and gravel to help with digestion. They are found in the wild in Africa, but are also raised on farms in other parts of the world. On farms, the birds are raised mostly for their skin, which can be used to make leather products.

3 A bird similar in appearance to the ostrich can be found in Australia. The emu is a flightless bird with an average height of five and a half feet. It is the world's second tallest bird. With its tall build and large eyes, the emu is a bird of imposing stature. Like the ostrich, it relies on its long legs to flee from predators. The emu is covered with dark brown feathers and feeds mostly on fruits and plants.

4 Deep in the thick forests of Australia and other nearby islands lives another unique flightless bird, the cassowary. The cassowary has a brightly colored neck and head, and its large body is covered with coarse dark feathers. The skin on its head is blue, with bits of red running down the neck. Cassowaries have a bony helmet on their heads that helps them cut through forest growth. It is the only bird that has a type of protective armor. The cassowary's best weapons of defense are the sharp claws that protrude from the end of its three toes.

5 The kiwi lives in the forests of nearby New Zealand. This shy bird is small and covered with brown feathers that look like fur. About the size of a chicken, the kiwi actually looks more like a badger. One of the kiwi's strangest features is its long bill with nostrils at the tip. The kiwi uses its unusual nostrils to seek out worms and insects.

6 There is one flightless bird that appears to fly—but it does so underwater instead of in the air. Penguins are believed to have lost their ability to fly millions of years ago. They now live most of their lives in the ocean. These birds look like

GO ON

they are flying underwater because their wings work like flippers, and they steer themselves by using their feet like a ship's rudder. Penguins can swim at high speeds in short bursts or at slower speeds for many hours. Some penguins can dive to depths of nearly 900 feet. On land, penguins waddle along clumsily on their short legs. They feed mostly on sea life such as crabs, shrimp, and fish. Covered with black, white, or gray feathers, penguins raise their young on land in large groups called colonies. They lay eggs that must be <u>incubated</u>, and both female and male penguins take turns keeping the eggs warm. These flightless birds can return to their exact birthplace even after they travel thousands of miles away.

7   Many birds have had difficulty surviving when people make contact with their habitats. Flightless birds are particularly <u>vulnerable</u> because of their inability to escape through the air. Several species of flightless birds, such as the dodo bird, are extinct because of over-hunting by humans. Others have found their habitats threatened by development. Still, many flightless birds continue to survive, amazing people all over the world with their strange and fascinating characteristics.

1   What is the meaning of the word <u>diversity</u>?

A similarity   **C** variety

B friendship   **D** loneliness

2   Which phrase in paragraph 3 is a context clue to the meaning of the word <u>imposing</u>?

A *tall build*

B *large eyes*

C *dark brown feathers*

D *feeds mostly on fruits and plants*

3   Based the meaning of the word <u>protrude</u>, what does the prefix *pro-* mean?

A two   **C** many

B forward   **D** free

4   Study the dictionary entry.

> **fea•ture** (fē´ chər) *n.* **1.** a distinctive characteristic **2.** the main presentation at a motion-picture theater **3.** an extra article or story in a newspaper *v.* **4.** to give special attention to

Which definition **best** fits the use of the word <u>features</u> in paragraph 5?

A definition 1

B definition 2

C definition 3

D definition 4

5 Which type of context clue helps you determine the meaning of the word <u>incubated</u> in paragraph 6?

   A example

   B contrast

   C synonym

   D restatement

6 Which definition of <u>lean</u> **best** fits the way the word is used in paragraph 2?

   A to rely on for support

   B to bend or incline in a certain direction

   C containing little fat

   D lacking an important ingredient

7 Study the thesaurus entry.

VULNERABLE	
adjective	
defenseless	*The lion cubs are defenseless without their mother to protect them.*
susceptible	*Children who are not vaccinated against chicken pox are more susceptible to the disease.*
weak	*Ken's weak shot in tennis was his backhand.*
young	*Young plants must be nourished in order to grow.*

Which synonym **best** fits the way <u>vulnerable</u> is used in paragraph 7?

   A defenseless

   B susceptible

   C weak

   D young

8 HABITAT : HOME :: predator :

   A friend

   B female

   C feathers

   D enemy

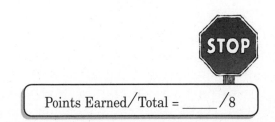

Points Earned/Total = _____/8

Mastery Test: Part 1

Estimated time: 50 minutes

Directions: Read the passage and answer the questions that follow.

The Tryout

1   The car slowed to a stop at the last traffic light before the school. The tryout was scheduled to begin in less than an hour.

2   "Uncle Sonny, I really hope I make the team," Rondell said nervously. "I've been working on dribbling with my left hand all summer, and my jump shot is getting more consistent."

3   There was really no way Rondell wouldn't make the middle school basketball team this year, Uncle Sonny thought. The young man had grown several inches over the past year, and he was becoming quite an athlete on the court. As Sonny pulled into the school parking lot, he pondered what to say to his nephew.

4   "Rondell, there's one thing coaches look for in every player. You need to be a team player and share the ball, because it's a team game. Use your skills to create scoring chances for teammates.

5   "I don't know, Uncle Sonny," Rondell replied as he opened the passenger door. "The team needs scorers, and I can either rain jumpers or go to the hoop. I could lead the team in scoring this year!"

6   "Close the door, Rondell."

7   Uncle Sonny thought back to his days on the high school mound. He had loads of talent, but it had all gone wrong.

8   "Check this out," Uncle Sonny said, pulling an old newspaper clipping from his pocket. "I brought this just in case you said something like that."

9   Uncle Sonny handed the article to Rondell, who looked it over carefully. It described a no-hitter thrown by a talented pitcher in the city finals many years ago.

There was even an action shot above the text, and Rondell recognized the pitcher immediately.

10   "That's you, Uncle Sonny! You threw a no-hitter? Why didn't I ever hear about this?" Rondell asked.

11   "Well, it's a long story. That was my junior season, and after that, I thought I had it all—a scholarship, pro scouts, everything," Uncle Sonny remembered. "I started looking out only for myself out there, and Coach didn't like my approach. I ended up quitting the team before my senior season even started."

12   "The coach let you quit?" Rondell demanded. "He must not have known very much about baseball!"

13   "He knew much more than I did, that's for sure. Rondell, baseball is a team game, just like hoops. After I quit, the team went on to win the state title. Everyone was looking out for each other, and they didn't miss their selfish superstar one bit," he explained firmly.

14   "I learned a lot that year," Uncle Sonny continued. "And I don't want you to make the same mistake I did. You have all the talent in the world, Rondell, but it's still a team game. You can't change that."

15   "I guess I see your point, Uncle Sonny. OK, assists are my game today! Dribble, pass, and create for teammates." Rondell exclaimed. The young man smiled at his uncle as he jumped out of the car and sprinted to the gym door.

16   Uncle Sonny looked at the faded newspaper article and sighed. "Go get 'em, big man," he thought, and he drove slowly from the parking lot.

1 Which statement best describes the theme of this selection?

   A Sports superstars look out for themselves.

   B Kids make mistakes.

   C Basketball teams need scorers more than jumpers.

   D It takes more than talent to be a great athlete.

2 Which statement best describes Uncle Sonny?

   A He is jealous of Rondell's basketball talent.

   B He loves and cares about his nephew.

   C He is a quitter who doesn't follow through on his promises.

   D He cannot admit it when he makes a mistake.

3 How does Uncle Sonny influence Rondell's decision about what to do during tryouts?

   A Rondell wants to give up when he finds out Uncle Sonny quit baseball.

   B Rondell is inspired to try to get a baseball scholarship like his uncle.

   C Uncle Sonny makes Rondell realize that he needs to be a team player.

   D Uncle Sonny's experience makes Rondell decide not to try out for the team.

4 Which character type from traditional literature is Uncle Sonny MOST like?

   A the wise elder

   B the evil villain

   C the magic helper

   D the silly fool

5 How does the difference in Rondell's point of view and Uncle Sonny's point of view create suspense for the reader? Use details from the story to support your answer. (3 points)

_____

_____

_____

_____

_____

_____

_____

GO ON ⇨

Directions: Read the passage and answer the questions that follow.

A Whale of a Surprise

1   Eduardo quickly scanned the poster, searching for the date of the festival. "It's this Saturday," he said to himself. "That should work." Cousin Morgan was coming to visit Eduardo for his birthday, and spending the day at the whale-watching festival together would be a perfect way to celebrate. He recalled last year's festival: The morning air had been chilly and thick with fog, and everyone had been quiet as the boat had churned its way out into the open Pacific. Once the first whale had been spotted, though, the entire mood of the event had shifted. People all over the deck had started yelling and pointing. Parents had held up their children to see. Eduardo and his friends had leaned over the railings to study the huge creatures that <u>dotted the green expanse of water like dark islands</u>.

2   Now Eduardo wanted to share the thrill of seeing those awesome animals with his cousin. He was sure Morgan had never seen whales close up before. Morgan and his family lived in Las Vegas, many miles from the ocean.

3   "All I have to do is convince my mom to take us into town to the museum on Saturday," Eduardo thought. "How difficult can that be?" When he reached his home, he lost no time in asking his mother if he and Morgan could attend the festival.

4   "Eduardo, I don't know," his mother said, scrunching up her eyebrows and turning around to look at him. "The festival starts early, and Morgan is traveling pretty far on Friday night. He will probably be exhausted when he arrives. That bus ride is long and uncomfortable."

5   "I know, but I'm sure he's never been on a whale-watching trip before. I bet he'll still want to go," Eduardo said.

6   "That may be true, but let's wait to make a decision. Your cousin is our guest for the weekend, and we want to make his stay relaxing and enjoyable."

7   "I understand. I just thought that it would be a fun thing to do for my birthday," Eduardo replied. His mom looked at him for a long time and then smiled.

8   "I'll see what we can do, but I can't promise anything."

9   Eduardo thanked his mom and turned away. He understood that Morgan would be tired, but he still wanted to share the festival and the whales with him. Eduardo hoped that Morgan's trip to California would go smoothly.

10   On Friday Eduardo was distracted all day at school. Twice when he was called on in class he panicked and forgot the question, and Mrs. Rusk even caught him doodling whales onto his binder. Luckily, the class was discussing <u>marine biology</u> at the time.

11   After the final bell rang, Eduardo jumped onto his bike and sped home. He arrived to find both of his parents home from work early, preparing for their weekend guest. They were discussing what chores needed to be completed before Morgan's arrival.

12   "Hey, what can I do to help?" Eduardo said.

13   "What? Eduardo, stop joking," his father said. "Your mother and I have a lot to accomplish before Morgan arrives, and there isn't much time."

14   "No, I mean it. I want Morgan to have a good trip out here. If that means cleaning, I can help," Eduardo said.

15   "That's a very nice offer. We just need to plan a little . . ." his mother's voice trailed off as she looked at her chore list for the afternoon. "Maybe we can work together to get things done here and then head out to the grocery store and on to the bus station."

16   Even though Eduardo hated cleaning, he cheerfully spent the next two hours washing windows and scrubbing the shower stall. He thought more about the weekend, and decided that in case they couldn't go to the festival, he had better come up with a great alternate plan. Sadly, the best idea he could come up with was to have a picnic at the community park—which was what they'd done on Morgan's last visit. He continued thinking on the trip to the grocery store and on the way to the bus station, but no better idea surfaced. Not more than a minute after he and his parents parked at the station, he saw a familiar head of curly hair through the window of an arriving bus.

17   "Hey, Eduardo!" Morgan yelled as he descended the steps. "Your parents called me to tell me about a whale-watching trip this weekend! I got some sleep on the bus, so count me in! Happy birthday!" Eduardo beamed at his cousin and looked over to his parents. They laughed when they saw the happy and surprised look on his face.

18   The next day the family was the first group to board the boat. When the first whale surfaced, Morgan yelled, tugged Eduardo's shirtsleeve, and pointed. Eduardo smiled at his cousin, happy that he could share one of his favorite sights with him.

---

6   In paragraph 2, the phrase "dotted the green expanse of water like dark islands" means—

   A a lot of dark-colored islands were in the green water.

   B the whales were round like dots.

   C the whales were big and dark in the green water.

   D the dark islands were shaped like dots.

7   Eduardo was distracted in school because—

   A he had not done his homework.

   B he was thinking about the weekend.

   C he was doodling on his binder.

   D he was afraid that Morgan would arrive late.

GO ON ⟩

8 Which summary best relates the important information in the passage?

   A Eduardo wanted to celebrate his birthday by going on a whale-watching cruise with his cousin. His parents did not say yes when he asked, but they made arrangements so the excursion could happen. When Eduardo saw his cousin's excitement at seeing whales, he felt very happy.

   B Eduardo convinced his parents to let him go whale-watching with his cousin Morgan. On the day of the cruise, after the family had boarded the boat and had seen the first whale, Morgan yelled, pointed, and tugged Eduardo's shirtsleeve. Eduardo smiled at his cousin, happy to share one of his favorite sights.

   C Eduardo did not know what to do for his birthday until he saw the whale-watching poster. He invited his cousin Morgan to come for a visit. Eduardo thought that his cousin would be tired from his long bus ride, but Morgan was up for a birthday adventure.

   D Last year Eduardo had gone on a whale-watching trip for his birthday. Eduardo wanted to go on the cruise again with his cousin from Las Vegas. Eduardo's mom didn't think Morgan would like to go whale-watching.

9 The author's choice of words in the last paragraph help the story end—

   A on a note of boredom.

   B in a surprise plot twist.

   C with suspense.

   D on a note of satisfaction.

10 Based on what he says and does, you can infer that Eduardo is—

   A impatient.

   B thoughtful.

   C selfish.

   D sleepy.

11 In paragraph 10, what does the term <u>marine biology</u> mean?

   A a member of the armed forces

   B an artistic style of drawing

   C the study of sea life

   D one who studies whales

12 How does the author use Eduardo's point of view to create suspense in the story? Support your answer with details from the text. (3 points)

_____

_____

_____

_____

_____

_____

_____

GO ON

Directions: Read the passage and answer the questions that follow.

The Road Not Taken

by Robert Frost

Two roads diverged in a yellow wood,
And sorry I could not travel both
And be one traveler, long I stood
And looked down one as far as I could
To where it bent in the undergrowth;

Then took the other, just as fair,
And having perhaps the better claim,
Because it was grassy and wanted wear;
Though as for that, the passing there
Had worn them really about the same,

And both that morning equally lay
In leaves no step had trodden black.
Oh, I kept the first for another day!
Yet knowing how way leads on to way,
I doubted if I should ever come back.

I shall be telling this with a sigh
Somewhere ages and ages hence:
Two roads diverged in a wood, and I—
I took the one less traveled by,
And that has made all the difference.

www.photos.com

13 What is the tone of this poem?

   A happy
   B excited
   C sad
   D thoughtful

14 The first stanza of the poem—

   A introduces the characters.
   B describes the speaker's conflict.
   C is the climax of the action.
   D gives away the ending.

15 The prefix *di-* as used in the word *diverged* means—

   A path.
   B come together.
   C two.
   D above.

16 What is the theme of this poem? Describe the images the speaker uses to convey this theme. Use examples from the poem to support your answer. (3 points)

_____

_____

_____

_____

_____

_____

_____

_____

Directions: Read the following haiku. Then answer the question that follows.

> Bare, broken, twisting,
> Are the stairs to happiness.
> Will you climb—or stay?

www.photos.com

17 Compare the themes of "The Road Not Taken" and the haiku. Then contrast their structure and styles. Use details from the poems to support your answer. (5 points)

_____

_____

_____

_____

_____

_____

_____

_____

_____

_____

_____

_____

Take a break. Then go on to Part 2.

Directions: Read the passage and answer the questions that follow.

The Supreme Court

The Supreme Court of the United States interprets the Constitution of the United States in order to review the laws and actions of federal, state, and local governments. All other courts throughout the United States are required to follow the Supreme Court's decisions. In this way, the Court guarantees equal legal justice to all Americans.

Supreme Court Justices

The Supreme Court is currently made up of a chief justice and eight associate justices. The first African American Supreme Court justice, Thurgood Marshall, was appointed in 1967. Sandra Day O'Connor, the first female justice, joined the Court in 1981. Once appointed, Supreme Court justices remain in office for life, and Congress cannot reduce their pay. These measures ensure the independence of justices and keep them free from political control.

The Work of the Court

The Supreme Court has the power to decide whether a law is <u>constitutional</u>. This power is known as *judicial review*. Most of the work of the Supreme Court results from its authority to confirm or reverse decisions made by the nation's lower courts. Because there are many cases up for review, the Court chooses to review only those it considers most important.

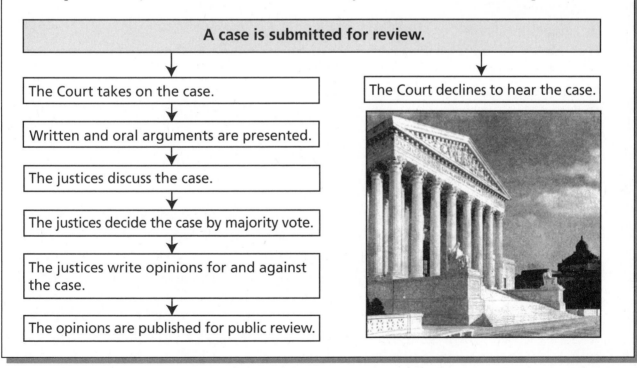

A case is submitted for review.

The Court takes on the case. → Written and oral arguments are presented. → The justices discuss the case. → The justices decide the case by majority vote. → The justices write opinions for and against the case. → The opinions are published for public review.

The Court declines to hear the case.

The Judicial Review Process

Once a case is taken on by the Court, justices consider written and oral arguments from each side. Then they discuss the case in private. When their private discussion is finished, the justices vote in reverse order of seniority. Cases are decided by majority vote, and one justice is chosen to write the majority opinion. Justices who disagree with the majority decision often write dissenting opinions, and those who agree can issue concurring opinions. The opinions of the Supreme Court are published in public records, which enables all citizens to study and review the Court's decisions.

The Influence of the Court

Throughout U.S. history, Supreme Court decisions have had important effects on citizens' lives. On many issues, the Court's position has shifted due to changes in membership as well as political and social factors. Over the past 150 years, the rights of women and African Americans have been both <u>undermined</u> and protected by Court decisions, and the freedoms of speech and religion have been extensively reviewed. Many Supreme Court decisions have caused controversy and debate, but this has only served to strengthen the Court's role in American society.

18 Which term best describes the structure of the text under the heading **The Work of the Court**?

    A cause and effect

    B comparison and contrast

    C classification

    D chronological order

19 What is the purpose of the flowchart that accompanies this passage?

    A The chart compares and contrasts the process of deciding cases.

    B The chart describes how justices decide whether to hear a case.

    C The chart outlines the steps taken in the review of a case.

    D The chart summarizes major cases of the past 50 years.

20 Based on the flowchart, what conclusion can you draw?

    A If a case is declined, only one justice listens to arguments for and against the issue.

    B Justices discuss a case after hearing arguments from both sides.

    C Justices must consider any case that is submitted to the Court.

    D Any citizen can submit a case for review by the Supreme Court.

21 Based on what you read, you can infer that—

    A Supreme Court justices rarely agree.

    B Supreme Court decisions are secret.

    C the Supreme Court's decisions affect every other court in the United States.

    D Supreme Court justices do not believe in freedom of speech.

22 Which detail supports the idea that the Supreme Court ensures equal legal justice to all Americans?

   A *Supreme Court reviews the laws and actions of federal, state, and local governments.*

   B *The justices vote in reverse order of seniority.*

   C *Sandra Day O'Connor . . . joined the Court in 1981.*

   D *The Court chooses to review only those [cases] it considers most important.*

23 Which detail should be included in a summary of the passage?

   A The Supreme Court interprets the Constitution of the United States.

   B Thurgood Marshall was the first African American justice.

   C Sandra Day O'Connor was the first female justice.

   D The first Supreme Court had six members.

24 Before they discuss a case in private, the Supreme Court—

   A votes on a case.

   B writes dissenting and concurring opinions.

   C allows its decisions to be reviewed.

   D considers written and oral arguments from both sides.

Directions: Choose the best answer to complete the analogy.

---

25 CONCURRING : AGREE :: dissenting :

   A majority

   B minority

   C disagree

   D opinion

Directions: Use the following dictionary entry to answer question 26.

> **un•der•mine** *v.* **1.** to excavate the earth beneath **2.** to wash away supporting material from under **3.** to subvert or weaken sneakily or secretly **4.** to weaken by degrees

26 Which definition best fits the meaning of the word <u>undermined</u> as it is used in last paragraph of the passage?

   A definition 1

   B definition 2

   C definition 3

   D definition 4

GO ON

---

27 The word <u>constitutional</u> in paragraph 3 means—

A *permissible according to the U.S. Constitution.*

B *a government in which power is distributed by a written constitution.*

C *relating to a person's physical makeup.*

D *an expert on federal law.*

Mars: The Green Planet?

1   Mars, often called the Red Planet, has long been the subject of scientific curiosity and science fiction literature. Mars and Earth have much in common. The two planets share several physical properties, including a day that lasts about twenty-four hours, a change of seasons, and the presence of water. Scientists now wonder not only whether life exists on Mars but also whether it can exist there in the future.

2   Currently, Mars is too cold and dry for life to thrive as it exists on Earth. However, scientists suggest that it may be possible to alter Mars' environment. It may even be possible to create an environment that can support life. Making Mars more like Earth would involve a process called *terraforming*. Terraforming is the manipulation of the atmosphere and the surface of a planet to make it fit for habitation by humans and other of Earth's life-forms.

3   The first step in terraforming would be to raise the surface temperature of the planet. Warmer temperatures are necessary to support life. Scientists have proposed several methods for warming the planet. One method involves introducing greenhouse gases to Mars' atmosphere. These gases would trap solar energy on the planet and would help to thicken the atmosphere. As the process progressed, plants and eventually animals would be introduced into the new environment. Ultimately, a human colony may be settled on Mars.

4   Some people, however, say that terraforming would be unwise because it may take decades or even centuries to complete the process. Those who begin the project would never see the results of their efforts. Others feel that it is wrong to disrupt a planet's natural environment because environmental changes on Earth have produced some negative effects.

5   These objectors fail to understand the tremendous benefits of terraforming the Red Planet. In fact, the benefits easily outweigh the possible drawbacks. For example, terraforming Mars could help solve some of Earth's long-term problems. A Mars colony could ease overpopulation or help preserve endangered species. Furthermore, introducing life to Mars would improve scientists' understanding of Earth's environment.

6   Some researchers suggest that the process of terraforming Mars could begin in a matter of years. The terraforming of Mars could become a reality during the 21st century. Even now, scientists are simulating what living on Mars might be like. Who knows? Mars might one day be known as the Green Planet!

28 In the passage, the writer's main argument is that—

    A colonizing Mars is essential.

    B Mars and Earth are alike.

    C globalwarming is real.

    D Mars should become a green planet.

29 Based on the article, which of the following does the author probably value most?

    A manipulating greenhouse gases

    B immediate results

    C disrupting natural environments

    D the survival of humans

30 Which of the following claims supports the author's argument in favor of terraforming Mars?

    A *Those who begin the project would never see the results of their efforts.*

    B *Mars and Earth have much in common.*

    C *One method involves introducing greenhouse gases to Mars' atmosphere.*

    D *Mars might one day be known as the Green Planet!*

31 Which of the following statements is a fact?

    A One step in terraforming Mars would be to raise the planet's surface temperature.

    B It is wrong to disrupt a planet's natural environment.

    C Living on Mars might be a lot like living on Earth.

    D Mars might one day be a green planet.

32 How does the author respond to views on terraforming that oppose his own view? Use details and examples from the passage to support your answer. (5 points)

_____

_____

_____

_____

_____

_____

_____

_____

GO ON

Directions: Read the following passage. Then answer the questions that follow.

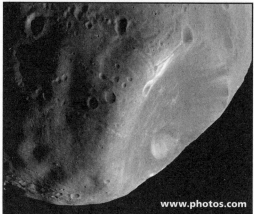

Scientists like Margarita Marinova are advancing our understanding of how to make Mars habitable for humans. Marinova was recently asked how fast Mars could be heated up.

"That depends," says Marinova, "on how fast we make the gases. According to rough calculations, if you had 100 factories, each having the energy of a nuclear reactor, working for 100 years, you could warm Mars six to eight degrees." At that rate, to increase the average Martian temperature to the melting point of water—it's about minus 55 degrees Celsius now—would take about eight centuries. Actually, it wouldn't take quite that long, Marinova points out, because her calculation doesn't include the feedback effect of the CO_2 that would be released as Mars got steadily warmer. "Devising more efficient artificial super-greenhouse gases will also make it faster," Marinova adds.

Thus, human habitation of Mars is a long way off. NASA's current plan for exploring the Red Planet does not include even a pioneering human mission to Mars. By the time a permanent settlement is established there—one that might begin the task of terraforming the planet—technological advances may make it possible to warm its atmosphere far more efficiently than is possible using the techniques being studied today by scientists like Marinova.

—Taken from the NASA Web site

33 Which of the two passages about Mars is a primary source? Give reasons for your answer. (3 points)

_____

_____

_____

_____

_____

_____

Directions: Consider the following statement from the passage "Mars: The Green Planet?"

Some researchers suggest that the process of terraforming Mars could begin in a matter of years. The terraforming of Mars could become reality during the 21st century.

34 Explain how the information given by Margarita Marinova disagrees with this statement. Which passage seems to contain more credible information? Why? Support your answer with details from the text. (3 points)

_____

_____

_____

_____

_____

_____

_____

_____

_____

Directions: Read the following passage. Then answer the questions that follow.

Nonverbal Communication Across Cultures

1   When you think about conversations, you probably remember things that were said. But do you remember facial expressions or the way you were standing? Probably not. That's because much of our body language, or nonverbal communication, passes unnoticed. In fact, we are constantly sending and receiving messages nonverbally. And as with other aspects of language, there are many differences in nonverbal communication among cultures around the world.

Body Posture

2   We can send messages with our body posture, or how we are standing or sitting. Overall, many people in the United States enjoy feeling relaxed and informal. In the United States, for example, business people sometimes use their feet to shut doors or move objects. However, in many cultures, it is a huge insult to show someone the bottom of your feet or to use your feet to gesture or move objects. Many cultures value formality and use their body posture to show it. For example, bowing is extremely important in Japan, and the depth and duration of bows are determined by the social status of the individuals.

Hand Gestures

3   Hand gestures can bring a lot of meaning to an exchange. Confusion or offense can result when the same hand gesture means something else in another culture, however. For example, in the United States the gesture used to bid someone to come to you is made by holding the hand palm up and moving the index finger in a curling motion toward your body. In a number of countries, including Taiwan, the Philippines, and China, this gesture is considered rude since it is the way that people beckon animals.

Visual Eye Contact

4   Visual eye contact is another important form of nonverbal communication. Among the people offering the highest amount of eye contact are people from the Middle East and Latin America. When Middle Easterners converse, they generally stand face to face and maintain eye contact. In some cultures, a lack of eye contact can be considered impolite and aloof. But in others, maintaining eye contact can be interpreted as disrespectful or threatening. Some cultures find it acceptable to stare openly at strangers. In the United States, however, people maintain what is called *civil inattention*[1] in public places.

www.photos.com

Personal Space

5   Proxemics is the study of how people use personal space in their interactions with others. Of course, how close people stand when they converse depends in part on the nature of conversation and the relationship between the two people. But it also is affected by cultural norms. What seems like a comfortable distance in one culture can seem crowded or standoffish in another. Most North Americans stand about 20 inches apart for a normal conversation. In South America and the Caribbean, certain people stand approximately 14 to 15 inches from one another when speaking. In the Middle East, it is common for speakers to stand only 9 to 10 inches apart.

www.photos.com

6   Of course, there are many nonverbal patterns that are shared throughout the world. And there are differences within cultures as well, depending on social status, education, and religion. Therefore, the examples given above should not be thought of as generalizations, but merely as ways to explore the different patterns among people of the world.

---

[1] **Civil inattention:** refers to the fact that it is acceptable to maintain eye contact in public places until you are about eight feet from someone. After that, people generally break eye contact by casting their eyes down or turning them away.

35 This passage is organized according to—

    A countries with unusual types of nonverbal communication.

    B stories of people using incorrect nonverbal communication.

    C steps to use correct eye contact and gestures.

    D types of nonverbal communication.

36 Based on the passage, what inference can you make about nonverbal communication among cultures?

    A Some cultures do not use nonverbal communication.

    B A gesture can have different meanings in different cultures.

    C People in Japan use more nonverbal communication than people in the United States.

    D Understanding differences in body language can help people communicate better across cultures.

GO ON

37 Write a summary of the passage. Be sure to include only the main ideas. (3 points)

_____

_____

_____

_____

_____

_____

_____

_____

_____

Take a break. Then go on to Part 3.

38 A verbal—

   A looks like a verb but acts like another part of speech.

   B is the past tense of a verb.

   C always ends in *–ing.*

   D includes a helping verbal.

39 All of the underlined parts of the following sentences are **verbals** EXCEPT—

   A My uncle wants <u>to sail</u> around the world by himself.

   B <u>Running at top speed</u>, I tried to catch the bus.

   C The most difficult part of <u>ice-skating</u> is getting up after you fall.

   D Because we didn't have any milk, I went back <u>to the store</u>.

40 Which of the following sentences is written in **active** voice?

   A The article was written by a well-known journalist.

   B The article claimed that several officials in an African country were involved in fixing the results of a recent election.

   C A recall of votes was demanded by the people of the country.

   D The article was denounced by the officials accused of tampering with the election.

41 Which of the following is written in conditional mood?

   A Did you finish writing your paper?

   B You must include at least four sources in your paper.

   C If you don't include four sources, your grade will be reduced.

   D Put your paper on Mr. Sahid's desk.

42 Which of the following is written in subjunctive mood?

   A Grab the dog before he gets away!

   B Did you let the cat out?

   C If you don't put him on a leash, he will run all over the neighborhood.

   D I wish I were a cat and could sleep in the sun all day.

43 Write the following sentence in active voice.

The anonymous letter to the school board was written by someone who is not happy with the current policies.

_____

_____

GO ON

44 Which sentence contains an incorrect shift in mood or voice?

A Go ask mom if she will give us some money.

B I wrote my favorite author a letter, and a letter was written by her to me.

C First choose a subject for you essay, and then write questions to guide your research.

D If I were rich, I'd set up a foundation to offer scholarships to needy students.

45 Which sentence does NOT include misspelled words?

A The witness couldn't describe the villin who stole my purse.

B Some experimental medicines are extremely benaficial.

C I abhor deceitful individuals, so promise you won't lie to me.

D The purpose of the safari was to study animals in their natural habbitat.

46 Which sentence is NOT punctuated correctly?

A Tony ordered milk pizza, and salad for lunch.

B After Maria saw the red dress, she knew she had to buy it.

C Mom made the salad; I set the table.

D My brother graduated from college on May 18, 2010.

47 Which sentence uses correct capitalization?

A Hilary read an article called "the new women in advertising."

B She was particularly impressed by a woman named Wendy lim.

C She learned that ms. lim had started her own advertising agency.

D Her clients include big companies like Wolfram and Liston.

48 Which sentence uses correct capitalization?

A Mr. Alexi i. Smirnov is a Russian.

B He emigrated to the United States through canada.

C The Communist party was still in power when he left his country.

D His wife used to sell Iranian and Afghan rugs.

49 Which sentence does NOT include misspelled words?

A The first fase of the project will be to contact influential donors.

B What an extraordinary performance that concert was!

C My cousin made a disastruous mistake during her vacation.

D Our neighbors have a particularly ferotious dog.

50 Which of the following sentences does NOT use punctuation correctly?

A Please take Juan to the park— nevermind, it's raining.

B Hmm—I can't decide which topic to choose for my essay.

C Well, I don't think Mom wants us to ride our bikes that far.

D "I'm so tired . . ." she said as she slowly fell asleep.

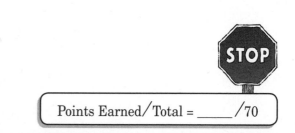

Points Earned/Total = _____/70

Keeping Score

	Points Earned /	Total Points	Percent Score
Tryout Test		/70	%
Unit One Practice Test Reading Literature: Key Ideas and Details		/12	%
Unit Two Practice Test Reading Literature: Craft and Structure		/10	%
Unit Three Practice Test Reading Informational Text: Key Ideas and Details		/10	%
Unit Four Practice Test Reading Informational Text: Craft and Structure		/10	%
Unit Five Practice Test Reading Informational Text: Integration of Knowledge and Ideas		/15	%
Unit Six Practice Test Language: Conventions of Standard English		/10	%
Unit Seven Practice Test Language: Vocabulary		/8	%
Mastery Test		/70	%

1. Fill in the number of points you earned in the Points Earned box.

2. Use the Finding Percent chart on page 144 to figure out your Percent Score. Then fill in the % box.

3. Compare your Percent Scores for the Tryout Test and the Mastery Test. See how much you've learned!

Finding Percent

Many tests give your score in both number of points earned and in percentages. This handy chart will tell you your percent score.

1. Find the band with the same number of points that are on your test.
2. Follow along the top row of the band to the number of points you earned. Your percent score is right below it.

Number of Points on Test

8

1	2	3	4	5	6	7	8
13%	25%	38%	50%	63%	75%	88%	100%

10

1	2	3	4	5	6	7	8	9	10
10%	20%	30%	40%	50%	60%	70%	80%	90%	100%

12

1	2	3	4	5	6	7	8	9	10	11	12
8%	17%	25%	33%	42%	50%	58%	67%	75%	83%	92%	100%

15

1	2	3	4	5	6	7	8	9	10	11	12	13	14	15
7%	13%	20%	27%	33%	40%	47%	53%	60%	67%	73%	80%	87%	93%	100%

70

1	2	3	4	5	6	7	8	9	10	11	12	13	14	15	16	17
1%	3%	4%	6%	7%	9%	10%	11%	13%	14%	16%	17%	19%	20%	21%	23%	24%

18	19	20	21	22	23	24	25	26	27	28	29	30	31	32	33	34
26%	27%	29%	30%	31%	33%	34%	36%	37%	39%	40%	41%	43%	44%	46%	47%	49%

35	36	37	38	39	40	41	42	43	44	45	46	47	48	49	50	51
50%	51%	53%	54%	56%	57%	59%	60%	61%	63%	64%	66%	67%	69%	70%	71%	73%

52	53	54	55	56	57	58	59	60	61	62	63	64	65	66	67	68
74%	76%	77%	79%	80%	81%	83%	84%	86%	87%	89%	90%	91%	93%	94%	96%	97%

69	70
99%	100%

WRITING TEST WORKSHOPS

Writing Test Workshops

To the Student

Why Do I Need This Book?

This book will help you practice taking writing tests. You will learn how to—

- read a writing prompt.
- get your ideas down on paper.
- write to tell a story.
- write to explain.
- write about an opinion.

How Will My Writing Be Scored?

Your writing test will be scored by test readers who use rubrics, or scoring guides. The rubric below lists 6 qualities of good writing. Read through each characteristic so you know how your writing will be graded.

Rubric Score: *1* is the lowest; *5* is the highest					
Ideas/Content—focuses on one main idea; the details add to the main idea	①	②	③	④	⑤
Organization—has a clear beginning, middle, and end; the order is easy to follow	①	②	③	④	⑤
Voice—communicates feelings and personality; the writing is unique	①	②	③	④	⑤
Word Choice—uses colorful, fresh words in the right places	①	②	③	④	⑤
Sentence Fluency—uses both long and short sentences that flow smoothly	①	②	③	④	⑤
Conventions—has few or no spelling, capitalization, and punctuation errors	①	②	③	④	⑤

How to Manage Your Time During an Essay Test

You may have 20 to 45 minutes to complete a writing test, so it's important to have a plan.

If you have 20 minutes,

◎ read the prompt, circle key ideas, brainstorm, and organize ideas. (5 minutes)

◎ write the essay. (10 minutes)

◎ revise, edit, and proofread (5 minutes)

How to Read a Writing Prompt

A *prompt* is the assignment for a writing test. The prompt gives you directions. It also tells you what to write about.

> ◎ **Step 1**
> Read through the entire prompt. Decide what the topic is.
>
> ◎ **Step 2**
> Read through the prompt a second time, underlining key words (*explain, compare, tell*) that will help you focus your writing.
>
> ◎ **Step 3**
> Look for key words or phrases you might use in your main idea statement.

Mina's Prompt

Here is a prompt for Mina's test. Look at the key ideas she underlined. These clues helped Mina understand what she is supposed to write about.

Prompt

Imagine that your state is considering <u>requiring all eighth graders to take an exam</u> at the end of the year. Students <u>will not be allowed to go on to ninth grade unless they pass the exam</u>. Write a paper in which you <u>present an argument for or against such a requirement</u>. Develop your argument by <u>presenting claims supported by reasons and facts</u>. Address at least <u>one counterclaim</u> in the paper.

The underlined words and phrases will guide Mina's essay. She will be writing a paper in which she must create an argument in support of or in opposition to a plan to require all eighth graders to pass an exam before going on to ninth grade. She must also address at least one counterclaim, or opposing claim.

Read the prompt below. Then underline the key words or phrases.

Prompt

Think of a rule or law in your home, school, or community that you feel is unfair or unjust. Explain the rule and why you believe it is unfair. Describe how you would change the rule to make it more fair.

I need to develop my argument for or against a required exam.

GO ON ➡

Argumentative Writing Tests

Review the Standards (W.8.1.a–e, W.8.4, W.8.5, WHST.8.1)

- Write **arguments** that support **claims**, using logical **reasons** and **relevant evidence**
- Introduce claims, acknowledge **opposing** claims, and present **counterclaims**
- Use **transitional words and phrases**
- Use a formal writing style
- Provide a concluding section

Some writing tests will ask you to write an **argument**. A good argument makes a **claim** (or claims) and then develops the claim with logical reasons and evidence such as facts and expert opinions.

Introduction

- establishes the topic
- states the claim(s)

Claim: *Offshore oil drilling poses too great a danger to our environment and should be discontinued.*

> **Use logical reasons rather than emotion to appeal to readers.**
>
> Good reasons—
> - involve safety or health issues
> - involve spending money
> - affect the most people

Body

- supports claim(s) with logical **reasons** and **relevant evidence**

Reason: *Devastating oil spills kill wildlife and pollute the oceans.*

Evidence: *The U.S. Fish and Wildlife Service recorded finding more than 6,000 dead fish, birds, and other mammals following the Deepwater Horizon (BP) oil spill in 2010.*

- acknowledges **opposing** claims and presents **counterclaims**

Example: *Proponents of offshore drilling claim that gas prices will skyrocket if we don't continue our current drilling practices. However, experts say that opening more areas to drilling won't have a huge impact on the price of oil.*

- uses **transitional words and phrases** to show relationships between ideas (*however, on the other hand, likewise, in contrast*)
- maintains a formal style

> **Relevant evidence is appropriate to the claim.** The following evidence is not relevant to the claim that offshore drilling hurts the environment.
> - Offshore drilling creates hundreds of jobs every year.

Conclusion

- restates main claim(s)
- draws final conclusions based upon the argument

Example: *Clearly, continuing offshore drilling will damage our environment. It kills our wildlife indirectly by disrupting their habitat, and it kills wildlife directly with deadly oil spills. In addition, offshore drilling takes America's focus off finding sources of renewable fuel.*

Kevin's Prompt

Below is a prompt Kevin was given on a writing test. Underline the key words in the prompt.

Prompt

Your community is considering building a skate park in response to young teens' complaints that there is nothing to do. Write a paper that develops an argument either for or against building a skate park in your community. Support your claims with logical reasons and evidence. Address at least one opposing claim with a counterclaim.

Words used in opinion writing prompts

- Agree/disagree
- Argue/argument
- Convince
- Oppose
- Persuade
- Point of view/viewpoint
- Position
- Support

Before writing his paper, Kevin used a chart to help him organize his ideas.

Topic: building a skate park

Claim: Having a skate park would be a positive thing for the teens in our community.

Reasons for	Reasons against
skateboarding is more popular than ever	a skate park would cost a great deal of money **Counterclaim:** Money could be raised through private donations
a skate park would cut down on damage to public property	a skate park would draw troublemakers **Counterclaim:** teens would be motivated to take care of the park since they want to use it
skateboarding builds character	
skateboarding is an inexpensive sport	

GO ON

Read Kevin's paper. Then complete the tasks in the Looking at Kevin's Writing box.

Kevin's Writing

Age 13–15 is a hard age. Your too old for toys but too young to drive or get a decent job. Sure, their's Little League and school sports to fill up the time, but the problem is they're organized. For the most part, you go to practices and games at set times. And inbetween? Kids my age need something to do randomly, something to fill in an hour or so, or to fill up an entire day. Having a skate park would be a positive thing for the teens in our community.

It's true that a skate park would cost a bunch of money. In these times of budget crunches, the city probably needs money for the police department, the library, and other programs. Spending money on a recreational facility such as a skate park could probably be put off until the economy improves.

On the other hand, a skate park would cut down on damage to public property in town, so it might actually save some money. Skateboarders are not aloud to skate on the sidewalk or in the street. So they go any place that has concrete! Sometimes that's down the steps of the public library. Or up the curbs of an empty parking lot. Anyway, skateboards are made of really tough material, so they don't break easily, that means they can cause damage too. If skateboarders had a skate park to go to, they would cause less damage.

Looking at Kevin's Writing

- Locate Kevin's main idea. Then locate his supporting details. Cross out any details that do not support the main idea.
- Does the order of the reasons in the body make sense? Renumber the paragraphs in the body to help build a stronger argument.
- Put a star by the opposing claim. Rewrite Kevin's counterclaim so that it is stronger.
- What can you tell about Kevin's personality from his writing style?
- Circle places you think Kevin might have used more lively verbs or precise nouns. Mark changes you would suggest.
- Mark and correct any errors in spelling, punctuation, capitalization, and grammar.

Also, skateboarding is more popular than ever. Adults are even doing it today. In fact, I read that it is now one of the most popular freestyle sports for men over 20. Girls and women are skating too. This town definitley needs a skate park.

Finally, skateboarding is a character-building activity, so a skate park would actually be good for this town. Skateboarding is a freestyle sport so skateboarders have to rely on themself, not on teammates.

In conclusion, our city should consider building a skate park. For one thing, skateboarding is becoming more and more popular. A skate park would cut down on damage to public property, and it would help kids build character. Most of all, it would give kids in the in-between years something to do!

Try It On Your Own

Now it's your turn to take a practice writing test. Follow the steps in order. If your teacher gives you a time limit, make a plan by filling in the amount of minutes you have to complete each step.

Time Allowed

_____
minutes

Step 1—Read the prompt. Underline any key words and phrases. (_____ minutes)

Step 2—Brainstorm for some ideas on another piece of paper. (_____ minutes)

Step 3—Fill in the organizer with your ideas. (_____ minutes)

Prompt

Imagine that your state board of education is considering making physical education an elective. Students would not have to take P.E. classes unless they wanted to. How would you feel about such a change? Write a paper that develops an argument either for or against P.E. being an elective. Develop a claim and support your claim with reasons and evidence. Be sure to include an opposing claim and counterclaim within your argument.

Topic: _____

Claim: _____

_____

Reasons for	Reasons against
	Counterclaim:
	Counterclaim:
	Counterclaim:

Step 4—Using your organizer as a guide, write your paper on a separate piece of paper. (_____ minutes)

Step 5—Go back and revise your paper. Then proofread your paper for mistakes in capitalization, punctuation, and grammar. (_____ minutes)

How Did You Do?

Now evaluate your own writing (or ask a friend to evaluate your writing). Complete the following tasks.

Consider This

1. **Ideas/Content** Underline the central claim. Put a star by an opposing claim.
   - Number the reasons that support your claim. Are the reasons supported with relevant evidence?
2. **Organization** Are the reasons organized logically? Yes _____ or No _____
   - Put a box around linking words that show relationship between ideas: *however, likewise, in contrast.*
3. **Voice** Does the writer communicate a positive attitude or does he/she seem angry or sound like a know-it-all?
4. **Word Choice** Circle any words that seem especially fresh or vivid. Cross out any words that are not exciting or precise.
5. **Sentence Fluency** Put a check next to any sentences that seem too choppy, too long, or sound awkward.
6. **Conventions** Check for any errors in spelling, capitalization, and punctuation.

Use your answers from the **Consider This** chart to help you fill in this rubric.

Rubric Score: *1* is the lowest; *5* is the highest					
Ideas/Content—focuses on one main idea; the details add to the main idea	①	②	③	④	⑤
Organization—has a clear beginning, middle, and end; the order is easy to follow	①	②	③	④	⑤
Voice—communicates feelings and personality; the writing is unique	①	②	③	④	⑤
Word Choice—uses colorful, fresh words in the right places	①	②	③	④	⑤
Sentence Fluency—uses both long and short sentences that flow smoothly	①	②	③	④	⑤
Conventions—has few or no spelling, capitalization, and punctuation errors	①	②	③	④	⑤

One way I can improve my writing is by _____

_____

Informative Writing

Review the Standards (W.8.2.a–f, W.8.4, W.8.5, WHST.8.2)
- Write **informative** texts
- Introduce a topic, previewing what is to follow
- Organize and develop the topic with relevant facts, definitions, and details
- Use **transitions** and precise language
- Use a formal style
- Provide a conclusion

When you write a paper comparing one movie to another or discussing the causes of the Civil War, you are writing to inform. Writing to inform is also called *expository writing*. **Informative** writing usually has the following three parts:

Introduction
- gets the reader's attention
- clearly presents the main idea:

  There are both good and bad things about playing on a school sports team.

Body
- contains relevant, well-chosen facts, definitions, details, examples, and quotations (the more specific the better):

  One of the best things about playing on a sports team is that you learn how to get along with many different types of people.
- is organized appropriately for the topic
- uses a variety of **transitions** appropriate to the organization (*most importantly, first, next, finally, in contrast*)
- uses precise language and specific words
- has a formal style, avoiding slang

Ways to Organize Information
- Compare and contrast—All the differences, then all the similarities or by details
- Chronologically— Events or steps in time order
- Logically—Least to most important facts or details

Conclusion
- follows logically from the ideas presented in the body
- ends with a strong thought:

  Overall, playing on the soccer team has been a positive experience, because even the difficult things have helped me become a better person.

Sarah's Prompt

Below is an example of an expository prompt that Sarah was given on a writing test.

Help her out by underlining the important ideas.

Prompt

Everyone admires someone. Tell whom you admire most. Explain why you admire this person.

Before writing her paper, Sarah used an idea web to help her organize her ideas.

Words used in informative writing prompts

- Compare/contrast
- Define
- Explain
- Summarize
- Tell

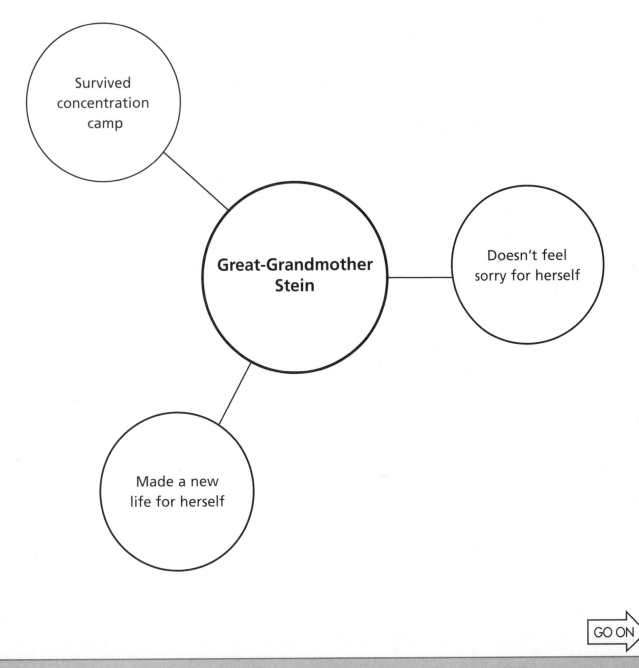

Survived concentration camp

Great-Grandmother Stein

Doesn't feel sorry for herself

Made a new life for herself

GO ON

Read Sarah's paper. Then complete the tasks in the Looking at Sarah's Writing box.

Sarah's Writing

To a lot of people today, World War II seems like it happened a thousand years ago. But at my great-grandmother's house, the war is still very real. On her wall, she has photographs of relatives who died at the hands of the Nazis—36 in all. On her coffee table, she has a scrapbook of newspaper clippings about the war. And in her mind, she has memories of spending two years in Treblinka, a Nazi concentration camp. The person I admire most is my great-grandmother, Sarah Stein.

First of all, I admire Grandma Sarah because she actually survived the camp. She was sent there when she was only 20 years old. She was in the camp for two years. She did hard labor 14 hours a day. She saw thousands of other prisoners die. But my great-grandmother made up her mind when she entered the camp that she would survive. She told me once that the secret to her survival was not to draw attention to herself. She kept her eyes down, did her work, and kept reminding herself that someday her nightmare would be over.

I also admire Grandma Sarah because once she left the camp, she was able to make a new life for herself. After the Americans liberated Treblinka, she

Looking at Sarah's Writing

- Label Sarah's main idea statement with an **M**. Label her supporting details with an **S**.
- Look for the following elements of structure: a clear beginning, middle, and end; topic sentences; transitions.
- What does Sarah's writing style reveal about her personality?
- Circle any lively verbs or precise nouns Sarah uses.
- Locate sentences that don't flow well. Suggest ways to fix them.
- Correct any spelling, capitalization, punctuation, or grammatical errors in Sarah's writing.

got a job. She saved her money and came to the United States when she was 25 years old. Here, she met my great-grandfather. They got married and spent their lives raising three kids and running a restaurant. I don't think everyone who went through what she went through would be able to do that.

Most of all, I admire my great-grandmother because she doesn't feel sorry for herself. She went through one of the most horrible experiences ever. She doesn't dwell on it, and she didn't let it stop her from living a good life. She told me that she keeps stuff around to remind her and everyone else what happened so that it doesn't happen again. Not so that people will feel sorry for her.

I admire my great-grandmother because she survived a concentration camp and made a great life for herself. I'm proud to be named after her.

Try It On Your Own

Directions: Now it's your turn to take a practice writing test. Follow the steps in order. If your teacher gives you a time limit, make a plan by filling in the amount of minutes you have to complete each step.

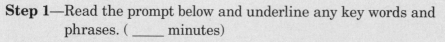

_____
minutes

Step 1—Read the prompt below and underline any key words and phrases. (_____ minutes)

Step 2—Brainstorm for some ideas on another piece of paper. (_____ minutes)

Step 3—Fill in the idea web with your ideas. (_____ minutes)

Prompt

At this point, you're probably nearing the end of your middle school/junior high years. No doubt younger students could benefit from your experience. Write a paper that explains how to survive middle school/junior high. Support your ideas with plenty of examples. Keep in mind that you are writing for students at approximately the sixth-grade level.

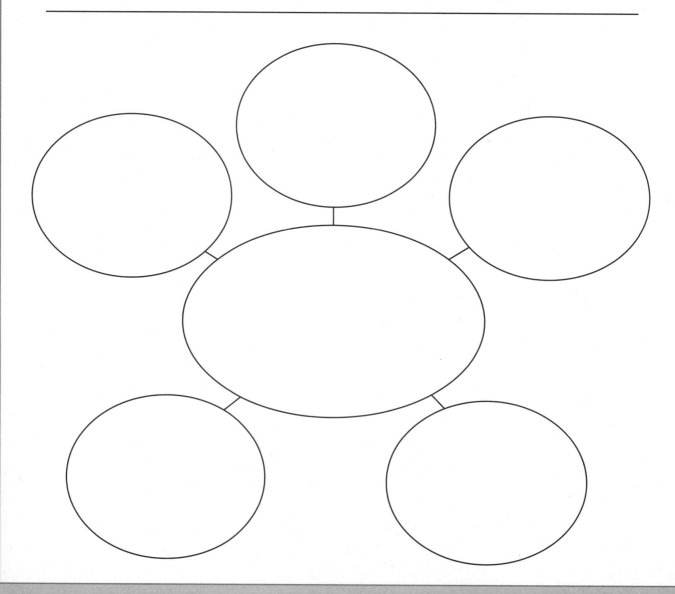

Step 4—Using your idea web as a guide, write your essay on a separate piece of paper. (_____ minutes)

Step 5—Go back and revise your paper. Then proofread your paper for mistakes in capitalization, punctuation, and grammar. (_____ minutes)

How Did You Do?

Now evaluate your own writing (or ask a friend to evaluate your paper). Complete the following tasks.

Consider This

1. **Ideas/Content** Underline the main idea.
   - Number the supporting details that support the main idea. (1, 2, 3, etc.)
2. **Organization** Are the supporting points arranged logically? Yes _____ or No _____
   - Put a box around linking words such as *first*, *next*, *second*, *finally*, and *also*.
3. **Voice** Put a **V** next to any part of the story where the writer's voice doesn't fit the topic or seems strange.
4. **Word Choice** Circle any words that seem especially fresh or vivid. Cross out any words that are boring or not precise.
5. **Sentence Fluency** Put a check next to any sentences that seem too choppy or too long.
6. **Conventions** Check for any errors in spelling, capitalization, and punctuation.

Use your answers from the **Consider This** chart to help you fill in this rubric.

Rubric — Score: *1* is the lowest; *5* is the highest					
Ideas/Content—focuses on one main idea; the details add to the main idea	①	②	③	④	⑤
Organization—has a clear beginning, middle, and end; the order is easy to follow	①	②	③	④	⑤
Voice—communicates feelings and personality; the writing is unique	①	②	③	④	⑤
Word Choice—uses colorful, fresh words in the right places	①	②	③	④	⑤
Sentence Fluency—uses both long and short sentences that flow smoothly	①	②	③	④	⑤
Conventions—has few or no spelling, capitalization, and punctuation errors	①	②	③	④	⑤

I can improve my writing _____

_____

Narrative Writing Tests

Narrative Writing

Review the Standards (W.8.3.a–e, W.8.4, W.8.5)

- Write **narratives** to develop real or imagined experiences
- Introduce a **context**, **point of view**, **characters**, and/or **narrator**
- Use **dialogue**, **pacing**, and **description**
- Use **transition** words and phrases, precise words, relevant descriptive details, and **sensory** language
- Provide a conclusion

When you tell your friends about something you did during spring break or write a science fiction story, you are narrating events. Good **narratives** have three parts:

Beginning

- engages the readers with an interesting **context** (setting)
- establishs a **point of view** (Use first person to tell your own story. Use third person if an outside narrator is telling the events.)
- introduces the **characters**
- may include a main idea statement:

The best vacation I ever had was the year my family and I went to Washington, D.C.

Middle

- presents events (rising action) that build to a climax
- uses transition words and phrases (*first, later, a few days after that*)
- uses **description**, **sensory language**, and **dialogue**
- has good **pacing**

Dialogue brings characters to life and keeps the pace moving.

Instead of writing, *My friend Keenan thought he heard a howling sound,* write,
"Uh, . . . Did you hear that howl?" Keenan asked with a quiver in his voice.

Pacing means how fast or slow the story moves. Use description and longer sentences to slow down the pace. Use dialogue and shorter sentences to pick up the pace.

Ending/Conclusion

- resolves the conflict
- may reflect on the significance of the events:

Because of my experiences in Washington, D.C., I have decided to pursue a career as a lawyer. I hope someday to serve as a senator in Congress.

K.C.'s Prompt

Below is a prompt K.C. was given on a writing test. Underline the key words in the prompt.

Prompt

Most people have an object they treasure: a piece of clothing, a souvenir from a special time, or a book. Tell the story of your most treasured item. How did you obtain it? What makes it so special to you? Describe the object in detail so readers gain an appreciation for it.

Before beginning to write his narrative, K.C. used the following chart to help him organize the events he wanted to write about.

Topic: most treasured item
Main idea: baseball glove from Grandpa
Event 1: pitched balls to me
Event 2: oiled mitt
Event 3: played catch with me
Climax: bought glove for me
Conclusion: Grandpa died but the glove reminds me of him.

GO ON

Read K.C.'s paper. Then complete the tasks in the Looking at K.C.'s Writing box.

K.C.'s Writing

My most treasured item is the baseball glove my grandfather gave me. My grandfather was a big man with a mane of silver hair and blue eyes that lit up every time the subject of baseball was mentioned. He instilled a love of baseball in me when I was only about five. He'd take me out in the backyard and pitch plastic balls to me, and I would stand with my Cubs hat on backward, hold the oversized red bat in my hands, and swing away. As I remember, I spent more time retrieving the ball from in back of me than Grandpa did from in front.

"That's okay, buddy," Grandpa would say. "You'll get the next one."

Sometimes I did, but most of the time I didn't. But Grandpa never criticized me. He'd just offer me gentle pointers that didn't always register at the time but eventually sank in.

Then, one morning when I was seven, Grandpa called to tell me he had a surprise for me and he was coming right over. I couldn't seem to sit still as I waited on the back steps for his big blue Buick to pull into the driveway. We lived on Oak St. then. When Grandpa came, I raced over to it and stuck my head in the open window.

"Here you go, buddy," Grandpa said as he handed me a sack. I could smell the leather before I even opened the bag. For a second, I was disappointed because I thought he had bought me a pair of shoes. Shoes are nice, but they're not really much of a surprise for a seven-year-old.

Looking at K.C.'s Writing

- What is the main idea of K.C.'s story?
- Locate the transitional words and phrases K.C. uses.
- Circle any details that are not relevant, or meaningful, to the story.
- Examine the sentences that reveal details about K.C.'s grandfather. Does he reveal these details mostly through dialogue or description? What additional details might he have included?

Actually I had just gotten new shoes the day before, so I really wasn't excited about getting another pair. My mom had bought me a sweet pair of Adidas. Anyway, then I pulled out the glove and couldn't believe it—it was so big! One finger seemed big enough to hold my whole hand!

"This is a man's glove," Grandpa said. "If you're going to get serious about this game, you need a serious glove."

We spent the next hour oiling the mitt because Grandpa said the leather would split if we didn't. As Grandpa massaged the oil into the glove, it crackled and creaked and filled the air with the rich smell of new leather. Then we went outside and played the first of many games of catch—with a real ball. Maybe it's my memory, but I can't remember dropping a ball that day. Or maybe I only noticed the ones I caught.

I've used my glove for almost ten years now. It might not be new anymore, but the smell of leather still fills the air every time I oil it. That smell never fails to bring back that special day and the games of catch with Grandpa that followed. I treasure the memories my mitt provides me. Somehow it makes it easier to deal with the fact that Grandpa is not around anymore. But as the saying goes, memories are forever. And I've got the glove to prove it.

GO ON

Try It On Your Own

Directions: Now it's your turn to take a practice writing test. Follow the steps in order. If your teacher gives you a time limit, make a plan by filling in the amount of minutes you have to complete each step.

Time Allowed

_____ minutes

Step 1—Read the prompt and underline any key words or phrases. (_____ minutes)

Step 2—Brainstorm for some ideas on another piece of paper. (_____ minutes)

Step 3—Fill in the organizer with your ideas. (_____ minutes)

Prompt

Tell the story of an event you experienced that you will want to remember when you are 80 years old. Describe the event in detail so that when you read the story as an elderly person, it will seem as if it happened yesterday.

Topic:
Main idea:
Event 1:
Event 2:
Event 3:
Climax:
Conclusion:

Step 4—Using your graphic organizer as a guide, write your essay on a separate piece of paper. (_____ minutes)

Step 5—Go back and revise your paper. Then proofread your paper for mistakes in capitalization, punctuation, and grammar. (_____ minutes)

How Did You Do?

Now evaluate your own writing (or ask a friend to evaluate your writing).

Consider This

1. **Ideas/Content** Underline the main idea.
   - Can you identify the setting and the main characters?
   - Write a **D** next to examples of good dialogue and description.
2. **Organization** Is the order of events easy to follow?
   - Place a **B** in the margin next to the beginning, or introduction.
   - Place an **M** in the margin next to the middle.
   - Place an **E** in the margin next to the ending.
3. **Voice** Put a **V** next to a section where the writer's personality shines through the writing.
4. **Word Choice** Circle three examples of sensory language. If you can't find three examples, look for places where words that appeal to the senses could be inserted.
5. **Sentence Fluency** Put a box around a section of the writing where both long and short sentences fit together smoothly. Write FLOW next to any sentences that seem too choppy.
6. **Conventions** Put a checkmark above any errors in spelling, capitalization, or punctuation.

Use your answers from the **Consider This** chart to help you fill in this rubric.

Rubric Score: *1* is the lowest; *5* is the highest					
Ideas/Content—focuses on one main idea; the details add to the main idea	①	②	③	④	⑤
Organization—has a clear beginning, middle, and end; the order is easy to follow	①	②	③	④	⑤
Voice—communicates feelings and personality; the writing is unique	①	②	③	④	⑤
Word Choice—uses colorful, fresh words in the right places	①	②	③	④	⑤
Sentence Fluency—uses both long and short sentences that flow smoothly	①	②	③	④	⑤
Conventions—has few or no spelling, capitalization, and punctuation errors	①	②	③	④	⑤

I can improve my writing by _____

_____

Research Report Writing

Review the Standards (W.8.4, W.8.5, W.8.7, W.8.8, WHST.8.7, WHST.8.8, WHST.8.9)

- Conduct short research projects to answer a question
- Draw on several sources
- Draw evidence from informational texts to support analysis and research

Sometimes a writing test or performance task will require you to conduct research and then write a research report. These types of testing events may take place over several days. You will be given time to go to the media center or computer lab.

A research report is organized much like an informational or argumentative essay.

Introduction
- gets the reader's attention
- contains the main idea

Body
- gives details that support the main idea
- contains good transitional words and phrases

Conclusion
- restates the main idea
- summarizes supporting details
- ends with a strong thought

Fatima's Prompt

Below is a prompt given to Fatima by her science teacher. Notice the main ideas she underlined.

Prompt

Conduct research on <u>robonauts</u>, robots created to assist astronauts in space. Explore <u>what robonauts do</u> and <u>how they work</u>. Gather information from <u>four different sources</u>. Organize your notes into a written report in which you <u>include information from all four sources</u>.

Evaluating Sources

Use the following questions to evaluate a source.

Are the writers experts or authorities on the subject? Does the author of the article or book have an advanced degree or has she spent many years studying the subject? Web addresses that end in .gov or .edu indicate that the source is from a government agency or educational body which usually has greater authority.

Who is behind it? Is the source from a business or group that has a reason for promoting some information and withholding other facts?

When was it written? The information must be up-to-date. Remember that some topics (medical research, technology) are changing rapidly so you must use the most recent sources.

Fatima turned the important ideas from the writing prompt into questions to guide her research. As she conducted her research, Fatima kept careful notes, including where she found her information. Below is a sample of her notes.

What are robonauts?

– Robonaut has a head, torso, arms, and hands like a person and weighs 300 pounds.

– machines that help humans work in space or go where humans cannot go (www.nasa.gov)

– "The newest model is called Robonaut 2, or R2. NASA and car manufacturer General Motors worked together to create R2." (robonaut.jsc.nasa.gov.)

How do robonauts help astronauts?

– could save time and reduce risks to spacewalking astronauts by going outside first to prepare work sites. (science.howstuffworks.com/robonaut2.htm)

– "Robonaut 2 or R2 . . . is the first dexterous humanoid robot in space, and the first US-built robot at the space station. But that was just one small step for a robot and one giant leap for robot-kind." (robonaut.jsc.nasa.gov.)

How do they work?

– have almost the same dexterity or the ability to make small movements as a human hand (science.howstuffworks.com/robonaut2.htm)

– "can be operated by remote control. An operator can use a headset to see what Robonaut sees through its cameras. The operator can then use controls to make Robonaut move." (www.nasa.gov)

Avoiding Plagiarism

Plagiarism is copying a passage directly from a book and using it in your paper without giving credit to the writer. Avoid plagiarism by paraphrasing, or putting information in your own words. As you take notes from your sources, be sure to put quotation marks around any passages you copy directly from the source. This will help you identify which information is in your own words and which is a direct quotation. Notice which of Fatima's notes are direct quotations.

GO ON

— "a person—either an astronaut or an operator at mission control—guides the robot remotely while seeing through its eyes via onboard cameras. The operator can wear gloves to operate R2's hands, or control R2's head motions by wearing a helmet remotely linked to the robot's head." (science.howstuffworks.com/robonaut2.html)

— Currently R2 is on a fixed pedestal inside the International Space Station (ISS). (robotnaut.jsc.nasa. gov.)

— R2 will turn on switches and replace connectors at the ISS. (science.howstuffworks.com/robonaut.html)

— "Eventually, R2 will be equipped with legs complete with toes that fit toeholds built into the station's walls, which will enable R2 to climb while leaving its hands free to carry equipment or perform tasks." (news.discovery.com/tech/robonaut-humanoid-robots.html)

What will robonauts do in the future?

— The hope is that R2 will be able to be programmed to do tasks on its own. (science.howstuffworks.com/robonaut.html)

— might enter dangerous locations on Earth in place of humans, like volcanoes and nuclear plants. (science.howstuffworks.com/robonaut.html)

— a four-wheeled rover called Centaur 2 is being "evaluated as an example of these future lower bodies for R2." (robotnaut.jsc.nasa.gov.)

— can explore other worlds (www.nasa.gov)

From her notes, Fatima created an outline. This helped her organize her ideas before she wrote her paper.

Main Idea

Robonauts are intelligent robots designed to help astronauts perform tasks in space.

I. What is a Robonaut?
    A. Humanlike machines that can help astronauts in space or that can go where humans cannot go
    B. Partnership with General Motors
    C. Recent robonaut—R2
        1. Has head, torso, arms, hands, gold helmet
        2. Is dexterous, can use hands and fingers to make small movements

II. How Do Robonauts Work?
    A. Remotely controlled by an operator who moves own hands or head, causing R2 to move
    B. Can do simple task on own with special programming
    C. Software can be updated to do new tasks

III. What Can They Do?
    A. Can assist astronauts with simple tasks
    B. R2 attached to fixed pedestal in space station 1.
        1. Undergoing tests—turning on switches and replacing connectors
        2. Eventually will be equipped with legs with toes to climb the wall of the station

IV. What Will Robonauts Do in the Future?
    A. Can conduct emergency repairs outside the space station
    B. Can be mounted on a four-wheeled vehicle
    C. Can explore dangerous volcanoes and nuclear plants

GO ON →

Read Fatima's paper and answer the questions in the Looking at Fatima's Writing boxes.

Astronauts of the Future

The suited figure slowly moves out of the space capsule. He makes his way down the side of the capsule until his feet rest on the surface of the planet. Slowly, he tests the ground, his legs moving slowly and steadily along the ground. His helmet turns side to side, as he surveys the landscape. He appears to be an astronaut, but he isn't. He is a robonaut, a very advanced robot developed to help astronauts explore space.

What is a Robonaut?

The robonaut program began in 1996 as a partnership between NASA and car manufacturer General Motors. The two companies worked together to adapt the robotic technology used to assemble automobiles for use in space travel. The goal was to create humanlike machines that can help astronauts in space or that can go where humans cannot go. The most recent robonaut is called Robonaut 2, or R2 ("R2 Robonaut").

R2 looks much like a human astronaut wearing a white spacesuit. It has a head, torso, arms, and hands. It wears a gold helmet and weighs 300 pounds. R2 kind of looks like C-3PO from *Star Wars*. Isn't that cool? Cameras inside the helmet provide vision (Hitt). Robonauts are dexterous, which means their hands and fingers can move the same way a human's can. The goal of the robonaut program is to create "intelligent" robots that can do some of the tasks that astronauts currently do ("R2 Robonaut").

Looking at Fatima's Writing

Find and underline Fatima's main idea statement.

Does the introduction get your attention?
Yes _____ No _____

Does the order make sense?
Yes _____ No _____

Circle any transitional words or phrases.

Does she meet the requirement of using at least four sources?
Yes _____ No _____

Cross out any sentences that stray from the main idea of the paragraph.

How Do Robonauts Work?

R2 is controlled by remote control. An astronaut or operator at mission control guides the robot using the cameras in the robot's helmet. At mission control, the operator places her hands inside gloves and moves R2 hands as needed. Head motions are controlled by wearing a helmet linked to the robot's head (Bonsor and Gerbis). R2 can also be programed to "think" for itself (Hitt). A controller can give R2 a simple task to do and R2 can figure out the best way to do it. R2's software can be updated to do new tasks (Klotz).

What Can Robonauts Do?

Currently R2 is attached to a fixed pedestal inside the International Space Station ("R2 Robonaut"). It is undergoing tests. Performing tasks like turning on switches and replacing connectors and other basic maintenance (Bonsor and Gerbis). In this way, R2 can assist astronauts with simple tasks. Eventually R2 will be equipped with legs with toes that will fit into toeholds in the stations walls. This will allow R2 to climb up the walls of the station while leaving its hands free to carry tools (Klotz). Can't you just see a robot crawling on the outside of the space station?

What Will Robonauts Do in the Future?

In the future, robonaut will be able to complete tasks on their own, saving time and money. For example, when something on the outside of the International Space Station breaks, an astronaut must put on a bulky suit to protect him from the extreme temperatures in space. It

---

Looking at Fatima's Writing

Are there any times Fatima plagiarized information? Write **Needs Citation** next to any passages where the source should be cited.

Does she use standard English and avoid using slang or informal language? Cross out any slang.

Mark and correct any problems in spelling, capitalization, punctuation, and grammar.

GO ON

takes astronauts hours to suit up just to go outside. These suits also cost millions of dollars ("R2 Robonaut"). Robonauts are built to be able to withstand extreme temperatures. In an emergency, robonauts could be deployed to quickly repair the problem.

NASA scientists have big plans for R2. NASA is developing a rover called Centaur 2 which has R2's torso mounted on a four-wheeled vehicle. This would allow R2 to explore rugged terrain of Mars and other planets. R2 could also be used to explore dangerous places on Earth such as volcanoes and nuclear plants. Perhaps one day R2 will be able to programmed to complete tasks without human guidance.

As humans continue to push farther and farther into space, robonauts will be there too, making space exploration easier and safer for astronauts. NASA described R2's arrival at the International Space Station as, "one small step for a robot and one giant leap for robot-kind" ("R2 Robonaut").

Works Cited

Bonsor, Kevin and Nicholas Gerbis. "How Robonauts Work." *science.howstuffworks.com*. N.d. Web. 20 Jan. 2012.

Hitt, David. "What is Robonaut?" *www.nasa.gov*. 1 March 2011. Web. 21 Jan. 2012.

Klotz, Irene. *Discovery News*. February 4, 2010. Web. 21 Jan. 2012.

"R2 Robonaut." *nasa.gov*. 30 August 2011. Web. 20 Jan. 2012.

Try It On Your Own

Step 1—Read the prompt below. Then underline key words and phrases.

Prompt

Your social studies class has been learning about Asia. Research the Great Wall of China. Write a report explaining the history of the wall, including how and why it was built. Include information from at least four different sources.

Step 2—Turn the information from the prompt into questions to guide your research. Write your question(s) below.

_____

_____

_____

_____

_____

_____

_____

_____

_____

_____

_____

_____

_____

Step 3—Conduct research to answer the question(s). Be sure to use the guidelines given in the prompt. Keep your research organized by including the source information next to your notes.

GO ON

Step 4—Create an outline with your main idea and supporting details.

Main Idea

_____

_____

I. _____

_____

_____

_____

_____

_____

II. _____

_____

_____

_____

_____

_____

III. _____

_____

_____

_____

_____

_____

Step 5—Using your outline as a guide, write your report on a separate piece of paper. Be sure to cite your sources when you use them in your paper.

Step 6—Go back and proofread your paper for mistakes in capitalization, punctuation, and grammar.

How Did You Do?

Now evaluate your own writing (or ask a friend to evaluate your writing). Complete the following tasks.

Consider This

1. **Ideas/Content** Underline the main idea.
   - Number the details that support the main idea. (1, 2, 3, etc.)
   - Does the report meet the requirements of the prompt? Yes ____ No ____
   - Does the paper include information from at least four sources? Yes ____ No ____
   - Write **Needs Citation** next to any passages that are missing a citation.
2. **Organization** Can you identify the introduction and conclusion? Write **I** and **C** next to them.
   - Put a box around transitional words such as *first, next, second, finally,* and *also.*
3. **Voice** Does the writing communicate a confident, formal voice? Yes ____ No ____
4. **Word Choice** Circle any words that seem especially fresh or vivid.
   - Cross out any slang or words too informal for a research report.
5. **Sentence Fluency** Put a check next to any sentences that seem too choppy or too long.
6. **Conventions** Are quotation marks used with direct quotations? Yes ____ No ____
   - Check for any errors in spelling, capitalization, and punctuation.

Use your answers from the **Consider This** chart to help you fill in this rubric.

Rubric
Score: *1* is the lowest; *5* is the highest

Ideas/Content—focuses on one main idea; the details add to the main idea; appropriate sources are used	①	②	③	④	⑤
Organization—has a clear beginning, middle, and end; the order is easy to follow	①	②	③	④	⑤
Voice—communicates feelings and personality; the writing is unique	①	②	③	④	⑤
Word Choice—uses colorful, fresh words in the right places	①	②	③	④	⑤
Sentence Fluency—uses both long and short sentences that flow smoothly	①	②	③	④	⑤
Conventions—has few or no spelling, capitalization, and punctuation errors	①	②	③	④	⑤

One way I can improve my writing is by _____

_____

_____